T

D1591556

The Copa

The Copa

Jules Podell
and the Hottest Club North of Havana

· · · · · · · · · **MICKEY PODELL-RABER** · · · · · ·
WITH CHARLES PIGNONE

Fabulous Food

Hand-Holdin' Music

NO COVER · NO MINIMUM · NO CABARET TAX

Collins
An Imprint of HarperCollinsPublishers

THE COPA. Copyright © 2007 by Mickey Podell-Raber with Charles Pignone. All rights reserved. Printed in the United States of America. No part of this book may be used or reproduced in any manner whatsoever without written permission except in the case of brief quotations embodied in critical articles and reviews. For information, address HarperCollins Publishers, 10 East 53rd Street, New York, NY 10022.

HarperCollins books may be purchased for educational, business, or sales promotional use. For information, please write: Special Markets Department, HarperCollins Publishers, 10 East 53rd Street, New York, NY 10022.

FIRST EDITION

Designed by Emily Cavett Taff

Printed on acid-free paper

Library of Congress Cataloging-in-Publication Data

Podell-Raber, Mickey.
  The Copa : Jules Podell and the hottest club north of Havana / Mickey Podell-Raber with Charles Pignone.—1st ed.
    p. cm.
    Includes index.
    ISBN 978-0-06-124099-7
  1. Copacabana (Night club : New York, N.Y.) 2. Music-halls (Variety-theaters, cabarets, etc.)—New York (State)—New York—History—20th century. I. Pignone, Charles. II. Title.
    PN1968.U5P63 2007
    792.709747'1—dc22

2007015252
07 08 09 10 11 ❖ / RRD 10 9 8 7 6 5 4 3 2 1

I dedicate this book to my three grandchildren:
Claudia, Luca, and Madison.
I wish they had known their great
grandparents, and also their way of life.

This book is also dedicated to the generations of children past and present who should know what an immigrant can do with his life and how he could shape the futures of many young hopefuls. It was the most exciting of times in New York and will probably never come again.

—Mickey Podell-Raber

Table of Contents

COPACABANA
NEW YORK

MINIMUM CHARGE

Eight Dollars Fifty Cents Nightly
Nine Dollars Fifty Cents Saturdays
(Per Person)

The minimum may be consumed in
food, beverages, or both.

Introduction

More than sixty years have passed since the original Copacabana opened its doors. Until now little has been revealed of the nightclub's rich history and the man behind its success, Jules Podell, my father.

Jules Podell's personal story is as interesting as the history of the club. His legendary reputation was well known, and he was both respected and feared by those who worked, entertained, or visited his club. Podell's unusual and compelling personality attracted a broad spectrum of characters that ranged from underworld gangsters to entertainers to a nun and her group of orphans.

The list of performers who played the Copacabana is staggering and spans decades, a virtual who's who of the greatest names in the entertainment business: Frank Sinatra, Dean Martin, Nat King Cole, Peggy

A postcard used for advertising purposes with a drawing by artist Wesley Morje of the Copa's most famous image; Claudia Podell would tell daughter Mickey that her image was the inspiration for the rendering.

Lee, Tony Bennett, Bobby Darin, Buddy Hackett, Jerry Lewis, Tom Jones, Paul Anka, Diana Ross, and the Temptations, to name a few.

The story of Jules Podell and the Copacabana reflects a truly unique time in American history when a confluence of wealth, relationships, and the burgeoning frenzy of American pop culture created one unique spot in which various classes (and races) mixed with the world's most influential entertainers, underworld gangsters, and sports figures to create a cultural phenomenon that was fueled by drinking, dancing, and amazing entertainment.

But it is also the story of my family and what it was like to grow up in the world of show business and bright lights and bright stars.

CHAPTER 1

The Family Podell

It all began in the town of Odessa; Nathan and Malka Podlubno lived there along with their two daughters, Minnie and Rose, and their small son, Julius. Odessa is a city of the Ukraine, which sits on the edge of the Black Sea. Catherine the Great founded the port city in 1794. Odessa served as a haven for Jews who were banned from certain regions of Russia but were free to make their home in the city. Because Odessa was open to everyone, foreigners of all kinds flocked there and it soon became one of the biggest cities in Russia.

Nathan and Malka Podell, Jules's parents.

From pictures I have seen and the stories I have heard, Malka, my father's mother, was very forceful and made all the important decisions; she was the head of the family. Nathan, by all accounts, was a gentle, meek, and mild-mannered man who worked in the town as a butcher. When he was not working, Nathan attended synagogue daily, as he was devoted to his religious studies and followed the teachings of the Torah faithfully. Malka was left to deal with the everyday duties of raising three children: Minnie, the oldest daughter; Rose, who had been born with a slightly hunched back; and the baby, Julius.

I know, from hearing the story, that one terrible night the Cossacks invaded the town of Odessa. I don't know the exact year, but the Cossacks were burning villages in Russia, trying to banish all Jews from the region. Men on horseback with sabers and torches went from village to village burning them down and driving the Jewish people from their homes. The Podlubno family was forced to flee their home and leave all of their material belongings behind. Minnie, who was only nine years old at this time, carried Julius to safety on her back as the family fled the terror. The Podlubnos found temporary refuge with a maid who had previously worked for them, who welcomed the family into her home as a safe haven.

While the Podlubnos were definitely not the wealthiest family in Odessa, they seemed to live a comfortable "middle class" existence. However, their lives and situation were forever changed once the Cossacks raided Odessa. It seems from that point on, the children's memories of their early years in Odessa were something they tried to forget and would rarely discuss.

The only mention of these past times would come from the oldest sister, Minnie, who constantly reminded Jules and held over his head the fact that if it hadn't been for her, he might have died. Jules, on the other hand, was grateful and always acknowledged that Minnie had saved his life during the Cossack raid.

I am not sure exactly how much time elapsed after the family was forced to flee their home in Odessa, but because of some hidden funds or a benefactor, the Podlubnos soon boarded a ship for a voyage that would take them to America. They were on their way to the "land of the free and the brave" to start a new life.

Upon arrival in the United States, the family quickly settled in the Sheepshead Bay area of Brooklyn, on Mermaid Avenue. Even today it remains the heart and soul of the New York Russian community. The neighborhood, near Coney Island, was full of Russians who had fled situations similar to the Podlubnos'. Although none of the Podlubnos spoke English, they were soon able to adapt and adjust to life in America. Through a friend of a friend, Nathan was able to secure a job at a local butcher shop near his new home. Since he was not the overly ambitious type, Nathan was happy to employ his skills as a butcher as he had done in Odessa. Although the job did not pay well and money was tight, Nathan was at least content with the situation. Once they had settled into a fairly simple routine, Malka and Nathan would have another child, a girl. My aunt Ann would become the only member of the Podlubno family who was born in America. I believe it was also at this time that the family Americanized its name from Podlubno to Podell.

Life in America was not easy for a family now made up of six people with a minimal income. Their standard of living was less than ideal at first, and it was a struggle almost every day. Malka would take odd jobs to improve the family's financial situation, but her main focus

The Podell family at a gathering in Coney Island, New York. Malka and Nathan are at the head of the table, with son Jules to their left. Jules first wife stands behind him to the right. And his sister Anne stands behind him to his left. Sitting next to Jules is his sister Minnie, while his other sister Rose, stands behind Malka.

was her children. Times were tough, but like other recent arrivals to the United States, the family was happy to escape the horrors of their homeland and relished the freedom in their new home.

My father, Jules, was cut from the same cloth as his mother; he had more ambition and drive in his pinkie finger than his father had in his entire body. This trait would become apparent when at the young age of seven, Julius decided he'd had enough of being "poor" and walked out of his school during lunch. The family would say that Jules never looked back from that moment. He simply quit school, abandoning a formal education for odd jobs in the neighborhood to increase his family's income. Young Jules would be educated in the streets of New York by those who were in a similar situation. Ironically, he followed in his father's footsteps for a brief period of time, working for the same butcher shop that employed Nathan. Jules would tell his mother that he was the man in the family and would someday support all of them. True to his word, in a few short years, he did!

There was never much said about my father's teenage years that I can remember except about his ambition and drive to make a better life for himself and his family. He would hand all of his hard-earned money over to his mama, Malka, to supplement his father's income and keep the family afloat. I believe it was at this stage in his life that he met and formed relationships with the people who would be instrumental in his later years as a nightclub owner.

All three of my father's sisters were very plain, stout women, as was his mother. Since the women in his family were not considered attractive, I believe, my father would develop a love for beautiful things, including women. My aunts all dated when they reached their late teens. Minnie was the first to marry and then Rose; both of their husbands were men from the neighborhood. My uncles were weak in character; it appears my aunts chose husbands who were very similar in personality to their father. It was their brother, Jules, who paid for their weddings and gave their husbands jobs.

Because of his hard work, ambition, and drive, by the time my father was eighteen or nineteen, he was able to own and operate his own butcher shop. Soon after that, he became involved with the operations of the Kit Kat Club. I remember hearing him mention that he had some type of ownership in the nightclub. It was during this time, through his involvement with the Kit Kat Club, when, I believe, he set his sights on one day owning a larger and more elegant nightclub. My father was making a name for himself, and through his connections and associations, he would soon be on his way to bigger and better things. From this point on, his family, especially his sisters, would rely on him for money and financial support—not just for themselves but also for their families. I never had the feeling the sisters had a deep affection for one another or for my father.

Sometime during this period, Jules also married. Since my father and mother never mentioned his first marraige, I was unaware of this fact until after his death. As I was going through some family pictures, I came across one that piqued my interest. The photo was of Malka, Nathan, Minnie, and her husband, Louis, some children, and my father with a young lady at a table in a dining room. Not knowing who the lady with my father was, I called my aunt Ann, his only sister who was still alive—she was living in Florida at this time—and asked her about the photo. Aunt Ann told me that the unidentified lady was a girl my father married before he married my mother. Ann explained that Jules

Seated: My father and mother, Dr. Max Som, Ethel Som, Uncle Sidney, and Aunt Rose. Standing: Aunt Ann, Dorothy and Jack Entratter, and Uncle Henry.

had married the girl because she was Jewish, and his parents were fond of her. It was strictly a marriage of convenience.

On the personal front, my father was conflicted and unhappy. He had met another woman, Claudia, at the time of his first marriage and was deeply in love with her. But Jules knew that his parents would never forgive him or accept Claudia since she was a "shiksa" and a former showgirl. So the story is that my father married another girl, and then, when his parents died a few years later, he had his first marriage annulled, enabling him to marry Claudia, my mother.

In my father's world, unpleasant things were swept under the rug and never discussed. Thus I never knew about my father's first marriage while he was alive. Neither did I know that my mother had been married previously to a man named Fred, from Texas, who had been sent to jail for some unknown reason before she married my father.

From my vantage point, my parents had a very strange relationship. My father was extremely jealous and my mother was extremely vain. My aunts would say that Jules had fallen in love with Claudia after meeting her on a golf course. Apparently, Claudia hit him in the head, by accident, with a golf ball. Knowing my mother, I don't believe it was an accident; I think she was probably looking for a rich husband. My aunt claimed my mother then had another "chance" meeting with my father, this one at a speakeasy. So once again she appeared in his life with her platinum hair and white chinchilla coat, and my father was intrigued and smitten. After these allegedly chance encounters, they began a courtship that would eventually lead to marriage.

Both my parents would have their previous marriages annulled. Since my mother was not Jewish, she converted to the religion for my father. My parents adopted me when they were in their late thirties and early forties. I rarely witnessed any public displays of affection between my parents; in fact, they did not even sleep in the same bedroom. My mother found what she wanted in terms of a lavish lifestyle and someone to support her. My father, in turn, had a beautiful woman who catered to his whims and looked good on his arm, something similar to a trophy wife, but there was definitely love between them.

My mother, Claudia Papineau, was born in Toronto, the youngest of twelve children from a poor Protestant family. Claudia would keep in touch with her siblings mostly by letters—I only remember visiting her parents once. I think the fact that she had converted to Judaism, to marry my father, kept her family at arm's length. They never approved of the "Jewish-Russian man" their beloved "Rudy" (Claudia's family nickname) had married. I do know that over the years my mother sent her family money and elaborate gifts without telling my father.

My mother, Claudia.

Just as my father was with his sisters, I wouldn't say my mother was close to her family. Her siblings never came to visit her; I think they were in awe of her New York lifestyle and were afraid that they might embarrass her. When my mother passed away, none of her family called or tried to get in touch with my children or me.

My father's sisters, on the other hand, all fawned over my mother. She was a beautiful woman who took very good care of herself and was regal in her manner. My mother would spend countless hours in the bathroom applying makeup and had a masseuse come to the house daily to give her a massage. She was extremely fastidious about her appearance, as if she was always on display. Her hair was auburn when she was younger and then she dyed it platinum blonde, the color it would be for the rest of her life. She was a perfect size six, and I don't remember her eating anything other than liver or salad. Candy and cookies were never allowed in the house, only the coffee maraschino-cherry ice cream that she liked. When I got older and craved chocolate or something sweet, she would point to someone in the street who was really fat and say "too many cookies." Her whole existence was based on her face and figure and that is all she thought about. *shallow*

My mother never spoke about her childhood to me. It was almost as if her life began when she married my father, the tough-talking Russian Jew. I do know that after she graduated from high school, she traveled to New York to do some modeling and she had been a showgirl in the Ziegfeld Follies prior to meeting my father. Clearly, she had the drive and ambition to obtain the glamorous lifestyle she longed for. My mother was very liberated for a woman living in those times; things were very different from today in terms of what role a woman and wife played in American society.

Jules had little time to devote to anything else besides his work and Claudia—in that order. I was a distant third. Again, although they were not your average couple, I do believe they loved each other. Each

Me as a baby with my nurse after arriving in Florida.

filled a need and void for the other and that was all that mattered to them. Each day, only a small fraction of their time would be spent together. As you will see, our family did not live what most people would call a typical or normal life.

I made my first appearance as part of the Podell family in February 1945 during a trip to Florida. I say "appearance" because one day I suddenly appeared; I was adopted. I would not know until several years later that Jules and Claudia Podell were not my birth parents. It wasn't until they had both passed away that I pieced together the following details.

At that time, the only one alive in the family who might know any details about my birth parents was Aunt Ann, who was now quite elderly. Her memory was spotty and she liked to drink, but Aunt Ann was my only source. I asked her if she knew of the circumstances surrounding my adoption. Ann said she was on a vacation in Florida, paid for by Jules, which included his three sisters and their families, during February 1945. My father rented a house, a compound, so the entire family could be near one another. One day a plane arrived with Jules, Claudia, a baby, and a nurse. One minute no baby, the next minute—presto!—a baby. No one in the family ever questioned my sudden appearance; nobody thought it was strange that Jules and Claudia had arrived with a newborn. Not a single word was spoken among the siblings about where I might have come from and the circumstances. The sisters and their families just accepted the fact that I was now Jules and Claudia's child. They had to, because if they didn't, Jules might get angry and stop supporting them. I asked Ann if she ever once asked Jules or Claudia about my birth parents over the years and she said emphatically no. I was not shocked by Ann's response. As I previously stated, in

My father and me.

My parents and me celebrating my second birthday.

My father putting on my party hat while celebrating my third birthday with a group of friends at our home on 910 Fifth Avenue. Close family friend and business associate Jack Entratter observes the festivities.

my parents' world, unpleasant things were swept under the rug and never discussed. My adoption and the circumstances of it would never be a topic of conversation within the Podell family while they were alive. I was given the name Malda—named after my father's mother, Malka. My mother hated the name Malka so they changed the *k* to a *d* and ended up with Malda.

From the time I was a very young age, Mother would always tell me "remember you are a Podell." That meant you had to be beautiful, you had to conduct yourself properly, and you could not show any emotion. After a short time I didn't want to be a Podell and live up to a certain standard of perfection. My mother's main standards were beauty and appearance. Don't get me wrong—being a Podell did have its advantages. I wasn't born with a silver spoon in my mouth, but I was raised to feel like I was. I never had to do anything for myself, let alone for others. We had servants and a staff; I would throw my clothes on the floor and they would pick them up. I had a buzzer in my room that I could ring for anything I needed. I would ring the buzzer and ask the maid to get me a glass of water, and it would be done.

There was a man working in the house who served as my father's butler, chauffeur, and valet among other things. John Jackson was his name, but everybody just called him Jackson. He would address us as Miss Malda, Mrs. Podell, and Mr. Podell. I was not particularly fond of Jackson and neither was my mother. I assumed my father liked him, or he would not have stayed in his employ. My father or mother would always say "Jackson, get the car," or "Jackson, drive Malda to school." John Jackson would work for our family until the day my father passed away.

When I went to school, Jackson drove me. This was always an embarrassment to me because the other kids would stare at me. Whenever anyone at school asked what my father did, I told them he owned a pizza parlor. I wanted to be like them, but I couldn't be. I had a hard time finding true friends because in the long run they all wanted part of the limelight that they thought I lived in. I was always a giving child, and I was always disappointed when friendships turned sour. I truly believed that other children lived like this. The kids at school looked at me with something close to awe, and I wasn't able to form any real friendships until I was shipped off to camp.

I have cloudy memories until about age seven, which is when my whole life changed. It wasn't until I was seven years old that I was told I had been adopted by Jules and Claudia and was not their biological child. I remember that moment as if it were yesterday; it was a complete shock. At that time we were living in an apartment at 910 Fifth Avenue, and every night my mother would supervise me brushing my teeth. The sink in the bathroom was too high for me, so I had a stepladder to stand on. I can remember the scent of my mother's perfume and her standing next to me. I was in a pair of blue cotton pajamas and had just started brushing my teeth. I'm unsure of the reason, but Claudia's anger stemmed from the fact that I didn't want to do something she had asked. At that point she said to me, "You are just like your mother. Keep it up and you're going to end up just like her . . . she was no good and neither will you be. I'm sorry I ever adopted you."

Stunned is a mild word for what I felt. I looked at her and asked her what she meant. She replied, "Apples don't fall far from the tree and you'll end up like your mother." It was all very matter-of-fact; Claudia told me that I was adopted, that she was not my real mother and Jules was not my real father. She then proceeded to say that I came from the "wrong side of the tracks," and with that, she walked out of the room. I never got over her saying that to me.

The next day I questioned her about my real parents, wanting her to tell me what my real mother and father were like. Claudia would tell me that my birth mother had died in childbirth, and my father was killed in World War II. At the time I believed her, and it wasn't until I was several years older that I questioned her story. Never once did my father mention in my presence that I was adopted. Once I discovered that I was adopted, my whole world changed. I would imagine that Jules and Claudia had kidnapped me and I didn't want to be with them anymore. I started to rebel over anything and everything I could. I'm sure that once I became a teenager, they would have gladly given me back if that had been possible.

I believe that Claudia wanted a daughter, and since Jules was accustomed to giving her whatever she wanted, he agreed to adopt me. My father worked long hours and was away from home most of the time; the majority of Claudia's day was spent alone in the house. I believe I was adopted as a companion and possession for my mother. She essentially wanted a little girl to while away the hours with her while her husband was at the club.

At one time I asked my mother why I couldn't have a brother or a sister. She told me she had had a hysterectomy years ago and was unable to have children. My mother proceeded to show me her scar; it was huge and she hated it. Back then, doctors were forced to perform hysterectomies through a woman's stomach, which was very painful.

Since many of Jules and Claudia's friends had children, they felt it was the respectable thing to do. I don't think my father ever wanted or needed children because his whole life was centered on the Copacabana.

A lavish party thrown by my parents at our apartment at 910 Fifth Avenue,
which was served and catered by the Copacabana staff.

The responsibilities of raising me were left mostly to the hired staff. My parents did not know what to do with me once I reached a certain age. They gave me as much as they could of themselves, which was not much. I guess in their world they felt giving me freedom without boundaries was a good thing. It could have been a lot worse; I loved them and they loved me the best way they knew how.

We lived at 910 Fifth Avenue in New York until I was about ten years old. The apartment was very dark, with wood paneling in the foyer and dark blue paint or flocked wallpaper throughout. Remember, this was the 1950s, so this type of decor was considered stylish. There was a doorman in the lobby and a creaky old elevator that would take us to the twelfth floor. I was scared to death of the elevator, never knowing if it might get stuck while I was on it. We had the only apartment on

My parents celebrating the holidays in 1947 with an unidentified friend.

the entire floor. Our maid was the only one who answered the door after someone was announced from downstairs. Once you entered, there was a long hallway and directly to the right was my father's room, which I was forbidden to enter unless I had been summoned. His den had lighter wood paneling and a desk and various awards on the wall. There was also a separate bathroom in his section of the house. My room was far from the main entrance of the apartment. My mother's room and mine were close but separated by the maid's quarters. It seemed as if my father's bedroom was at least two football fields away from us.

The building was very old and had a circular driveway where I would sometimes roller-skate. One day I fell after I stopped short on my skates and landed on my elbows. I took a hard spill onto sharp gravel, which stuck in my arms. I remember crying all the way to our apartment because of the terrible pain. My parents never expressed any emotion. I never saw my mother or father cry in front of me as a child. This was hard for me since I was a very emotional person, and it was hard to bond emotionally with them.

My mother's daily routine seldom varied. She would generally awake at nine-thirty in the morning and then get herself ready, make-upwise, before she would appear from her bedroom. Between then and 3 P.M., which was time to have lunch with my father, she'd find things to occupy herself with. To prepare for lunch, she would instruct the servants what to do, what special food to make, or have them call in an order from Farber's. My father liked Farber's sturgeon and herring. My mother's lunch tray consisted of melba toast with cottage cheese and possibly one pear. They would sit in his den and eat lunch before he got ready to leave for the club. I assume that at some point during the day

My mother with our dog, Tinker. Tinker was a given to us by Sammy Davis Jr.

she visited the beauty parlor or went shopping. She would have her hair done or shop at least three to four times a week. Her exercise consisted of yoga that she would practice in her room; I'd sometimes walk by and she would be standing on her head.

Dad's everyday routine never varied; he probably did not get up until one in the afternoon. Then he would proceed to work in his den until it was time for lunch with my mother. As a rule, he usually had a massage at home three times a week and then he'd get dressed and Jackson would drive him to the Copa. Jackson would then return to the house to do odd jobs or run errands. Sometime around 4 A.M. Jackson would return to the Copa to pick my father up. I don't believe my father came home before 4 A.M. except on a few rare occasions.

We had a long dining-room table, worthy of a King, and I would sit at one end and my mother at the other. The table had a buzzer underneath it that my mother would buzz, letting the maid know it was now time to serve dinner. The meals were of three courses, even if we ordered from the club. There was a red phone in my father's office, which was the hotline directly to the Copa kitchen, and my mother and I would call and order off the Copa menu at least three or four times a week. I don't ever recall my mother cooking in our kitchen at the house; it just was not something she did. Since she was so fanatical about her weight, she tried to stay away from fattening foods. We'd start off with a salad or vichyssoise and then it was liver, chicken, or steak with vegetables for the main course. She was not a big eater and would encourage me not to eat a lot so I could be thin like she was.

Since this was the environment I grew up in, I assumed that everyone lived like we did. Believe me when I tell you that I was in shock to find out that other people didn't have maids to serve them. I was never even in a grocery store until after I got married because my mother had everything delivered to the house or the staff would go and buy it for us.

Very rarely did mother venture out during weeknights. I remember one time she kissed me good-bye—I can still smell her perfume—and told me that they were going to be on *The Ed Sullivan Show*. She told me what channel to watch, if I wanted to, so I could look for them in the audience. Well, there I was sitting alone in my room and I see her, in a white mink stole, and my dad being introduced by Ed Sullivan on television.

The one thing I looked forward to every year was going to camp for eight weeks during the summer months. I enjoyed being away from the hustle and bustle of the city, and because nothing was expected of me, I could be myself. I also enjoyed being with the other children. Through the years I went to several camps located in Massachusetts or Vermont that catered to Jewish children. At camp I played archery, went swimming and horseback riding. I would be disappointed when the time was over because I had friends, companionship, and was able to be around people my own age with the same interests. In fact, I still keep in touch with one of the girls I went to camp with back then.

On parents' day one year, my father and mother came to visit me at camp. I was embarrassed because all the other parents were in shorts and casual clothes, but my father had on a dress shirt and slacks with a sport jacket. I remember he complained the whole time because he was hot, uncomfortable, and sweating. It was summer, this was a camp, and there was no air-conditioning . . . I don't know what he expected. My parents also had Jackson bring baskets of food for them.

This also proved to be embarrassing because everyone else was eating the food provided by the camp and here we were with these gourmet lunches. I still have a picture of my parents sitting on a log eating their lunch. This was the only time he ever came to visit me during all my years of being at camp.

It sounds funny now, but I really just wanted to be a normal kid with normal parents who weren't involved in show business. But that wasn't our life. I was Jules Podell's daughter and that connected us to the big world of New York City nightlife, and when I look back at all the wonderful people I got to see in their heyday, there isn't much I would wish to change.

*My father visiting me
at summer camp
during my teen years.*

CHAPTER 2

The Opening of the Copa

In 1920, Prohibition began in the United States after a constitutional amendment was passed. From January 16, 1920, until December 5, 1933, the "manufacture, sale, or transportation of intoxicating liquors within, the importation thereof into, or the exportation thereof from the United States and all territory subject to the jurisdiction thereof for beverage purposes" was prohibited in the United States.

Supporters of the law suggested that Prohibition would serve to reduce corruption and crime in the United States. In these terms, Prohibition was a failure, since the law only led to an increase in crime and made those who did sell and supply liquor rich and powerful.

The famous Copacabana Girl drawing by Wesley Morje.

The line outside the Copacabana during prom season. Taking your date to the Copa after the prom became a long-standing tradition for students in the New York–New Jersey area.

You can imagine the effect the new law had on the bar, nightclub, and saloon trade. It was said that for every legitimate bar that closed, a dozen speakeasies opened. Speakeasies would emerge as a refuge where patrons could go to consume alcohol and be entertained. Since speakeasies were illegal, patrons were usually given a password to gain entrance. Organized crime owned and supplied these illegal clubs with liquor and protection from the law. Local law enforcement agencies turned a blind eye to such criminal operations in exchange for bribes.

When Prohibition ended, the organized-crime outfits that had run the majority of speakeasies did not want to give up the lucrative profits the clubs had generated. They therefore needed front men, so-called legitimate businessmen, to act as owners of the legitimate bars and clubs. In many cases, the men selected would be owners in name only. While these front men operated the clubs, the mob skimmed profits from the nightly take and essentially oversaw the entire operation of the establishment.

The Copacabana opened its doors in October 1940. The nightclub was located in the basement of the Hotel Fourteen, and the official address was 10 East Sixtieth Street. This location had previously housed a nightclub and restaurant called the Villa Vallee, which was owned by the then-famous crooner Rudy Vallee. Vallee became famous in vaudeville, radio, and the movies before newcomer Bing Crosby eclipsed his popularity in the mid-1930s.

Monte Proser's name appeared on the lease as the primary owner when the Copacabana first opened its doors, as it also did on the menus, matchbooks, handbills, and the club's outside awning. Proser had made a name for himself as a nightclub publicist, with one of his accounts being the famed Stork Club. The Stork Club, owned by Sherman Billingsley,

COPACABANA DINNER

(Price of Entree Determines Cost of Complete Dinner)

Hors d'Oeuvres

SUPREME OF FRUIT, MAISON
CHILLED CLAM JUICE   CHERRYSTONE CLAM COCKTAIL
CHOPPED CHICKEN LIVERS, COPA   ROYAL CHINOOK SALMON
CHILLED VEGETABLE, TOMATO OR GRAPEFRUIT JUICE
FILET OF HERRING WITH SOUR CREAM
CHILLED HALF GRAPEFRUIT

10 East 60th

Potages

Cream of Peas, Croutons   Consomme Fermiere
            French Onion Soup

Entrees

DEEP SEA SCALLOPS, SAUTE AMANDINES	6.45
BROILED IMPORTED LOBSTER TAILS, GARLIC BUTTER	9.15
HALF SPRING CHICKEN EN CASSEROLE, NICOISE	7.10
PRIME SALISBURY STEAK, SAUCE CHAMPIGNON	7.05
BAKED HAM, CANDIED YAM, GRAND MARNIER	7.60
LONG ISLAND DUCKLING, BIGARADE WITH APPLE SAUCE	7.90
CHICKEN LIVERS ANGLAISE ON TOAST	7.50
SHASHLIK COPACABANA, GARNI	7.75
BRAISED SHORT RIBS OF PRIME BEEF, JARDINIERE	7.05
SAUTEED SCALLOPINES OF VEAL, HUNTER'S STYLE	7.75
BROILED PRIME FILET MIGNON	10.50
PRIME RIBS OF BEEF AU JUS	9.30
PRIME TOURNEDOS, PETITE ONIONS GLACE	9.40
BEEF STROGANOFF A LA RUSSE ON TOAST	9.30
TIPS OF TENDERLOIN A LA PODELL, RICE PILAFF	9.25
MINUTE STEAK SAUTE WITH SMOTHERED ONIONS	9.50
ROAST STUFFED TOM TURKEY WITH GIBLET GRAVY, CRANBERRY SAUCE AND CANDIED YAM	7.40

FROM OUR CHINESE KITCHEN

WHITE MEAT CHICKEN CHOW MEIN WITH WATER CHESTNUTS, MUSHROOMS AND BAMBOO SHOOTS	7.40
GREEN PEPPER STEAK WITH BAMBOO SHOOTS, WATER CHESTNUTS, MUSHROOMS AND FRESH TOMATOES	7.35

ROLLS and BUTTER

Legumes

Garden Green Peas   Mixed Green Salad   Pomme Copacabana

Desserts

COFFEE CAKE   BLUEBERRY PIE   CHILLED HALF GRAPEFFUIT
ICE CREAM CAKE   FRUIT JELLO WITH WHIPPED CREAM   FRUIT COMPOTE
CAMEMBERT CHEESE   APPLE PIE   LEMON OR RASPBERRY SHERBET
SPUMONI   CHOCOLATE, STRAWBERRY, VANILLA OR COFFEE ICE CREAM
COFFEE   TEA   or   MILK

NO SUBSTITUTIONS
We are compelled by law to collect 6% New York State Tax
Wednesday, April 29, 1970   (Served till 10 P. M.)

The dinner menu at the Copacabana from April 29, 1970. Besides the headline entertainment, the food at the club was also world famous.

was located at 3 East Fifty-third Street in New York. In the 1930s, the Stork Club was "the New Yorkiest spot in New York" according to columnist Walter Winchell. Also joining Proser to run the club was my father and Jack Entratter.

Monte Proser knew Jack Entratter, as they had both worked at the Stork Club. Entratter, who was in his mid-twenties when the Copa first opened, would stay at the club for over a decade before heading to Las Vegas. Entratter was a large man, six foot three, and an imposing figure, which helped him begin his career in the New York clubs as a bouncer. Through his connections and outgoing personality, Entratter was able to cultivate friendships with the top people who ran the nightclubs. By most accounts, Entratter was a very religious and family-oriented man who loved children and for the most part had a gentle demeanor and even temper.

Proser would also venture out to California and became part owner of La Conga, a nightclub in Hollywood. Within a short period of time, Proser would also open various nightspots in others cities such as Miami Beach, Boston, and New York. While this proved lucrative in many cases, it also stretched Proser thin in terms of the attention he could focus on each nightspot. My father and Jack Entratter essentially ran the day-to-day operation of the Copacabana although Monte Proser's name was out front.

Monte Proser and company spared no expense when they decided on a theme that mixed Latin and tropical influences for the Copacabana decor. Interior designer Clark Robinson, who had worked on other venues with Proser, was hired to transform the space into an elegant nightspot. In a few months Robinson's transformation would be complete; it was extraordinary and exciting. To this day, those who remember visiting the Copacabana mention the lush tropical motifs and palm trees that decorated the club.

When it first opened its doors, the outside of the Copacabana had an awning from the front steps to the street that initially read MONTE PROSER'S COPACABANA with the address—10 E. 60—above. A few years later, another awning would be added, announcing that the club—now open in the summer—had installed ARMO AIR CONDITIONING. During the first few years of operation, the club shut down during the summer season for several months.

Phoebe Jacobs recalls:

> I was a teenager the first time I stepped into the Copacabana. My father would take me to all the places of entertainment and music in and around New York. I was a music lover from the time I was about twelve years old. Well, the first time I went to the Copa, I was fascinated by the palm trees and the silk coconuts. The Copa had a real feel and flavor of South America. I later was told that the decor was similar to the Rio, a very famous club in Rio de Janeiro. I was extraordinarily impressed, as any teenager would be, although I had gone to many nightclubs. My uncle was Ralph Watkins, so I knew about nightclubs. Ralph had opened a place called Kelly's Stable, which was when Fifty-second Street started to be called the Swing Street, and he hired entertainment like Billie Holliday, Nat King Cole, Billy Eckstine, and Billy Daniels. Back then Fifty-second Street was jumping with all kinds of music and things. Later Ralph had the Royal Roost, Bop City, and Basin Street East among others. So I was very aware of the nightclub scene and it took a lot to impress me. Well, I was impressed by the Copa!

The first chef hired to run the kitchens at the new nightclub was Pedro Pujal. Pujal had gained acclaim as the head chef of the Terrace

My father and a friend cooking up something in the Copa kitchen.

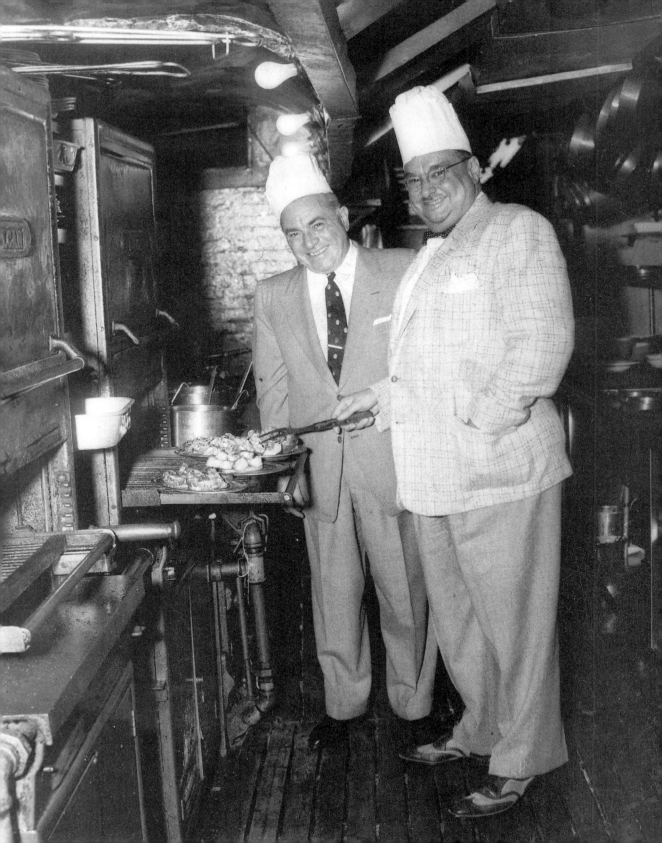

Club at the 1939 New York World's Fair. Approximately fifty people were hired to fill staff positions as cooks, bartenders, waiters, and other key personnel. My father prided himself on the cuisine served at the club and spent most of his time in the kitchen supervising the chefs and waitstaff.

Robert Alton and Margery Fielding were hired as choreographers for the first revue that would open at the Copacabana. Alton and Fielding rehearsed the line of dancing girls, originally dubbed the Samba Sirens, for weeks before the club's opening so they would be in top shape for their debut. My father would soon change the name of the Samba Sirens to the more appropriate Copa Girls.

Although it appeared to the press and public that Monte Proser owned the Copacabana, insiders knew that Frank Costello was the main money and muscle behind the scenes. Costello and his associates facilitated in getting the club off the ground with the proper connections for a successful start. Says music agent Frank Military: "Monte Proser fronted the club in the beginning while Jules Podell and Jack Entratter were managing and running it. The word on the street was that Frank Costello had a piece of the Copa. But Podell was the one who ran the day-to-day operations of the club."

Frank Costello was born Francesco Castiglia on January 26, 1891, in Calabria, Italy. At the age of four, he, along with his mother and brother, arrived in the United States. Costello would become one of the most powerful and influential organized-crime bosses in American history during the 1940s and 1950s. At one point during his reign, he was so powerful that his nickname was the "Prime Minister of the Underworld." Costello was associated with the Genovese crime family and based out of New York.

It was not until 1957, after a power struggle that culminated in an assassination attempt on Costello by Vito Genovese, that Costello would lose control and power of his organized-crime rackets, including his interest in the Copacabana. Even though the hit on Costello failed, Genovese appointed himself as acting boss. After Costello recovered, Genovese agreed to leave him alone if he would cede all of his organized-crime interests and no longer be involved with the Genovese family's businesses. It is not known who, if anyone, was then involved with the Copacabana on a regular basis as Costello had been. Costello would remain a New Yorker until he passed away in 1973 from a heart attack.

Costello and his people obviously had an arrangement before the Copacabana opened with Proser; what their exact arrangement was remains unclear. What is clear to many is that Frank Costello and the Genovese family had a major investment and interest in the ownership and involvement of the Copa.

From all the opening-month reviews, it seemed the Copacabana was a smash among critics and columnists, who praised its uniqueness and decor. The *New York Sun* raved, "The Copacabana is definitely a smart spot and unlike anything else the town has to offer in decor and atmosphere. The club has been crowded nightly since its opening . . . if this pace continues, the club's place in this hit class can scarcely be disputed."

Although Jules Podell had previously operated a Coney Island restaurant, a Fulton Street chophouse, and the Kit Kat Club, it was the Copacabana that would be his lifelong passion. As 1940 ended, a new era was dawning for the world of nightclubs and the Copacabana was leading the way. My father's life would change forever as the Copacabana went on to become the most famous nightclub in the world.

Every Sunday night my mother and I would go to the Copa for dinner and the early show. At three in the afternoon we'd start getting ready and dress up for our evening at the club. We would not leave until five or so, as it took my mother at least two hours to get herself together. She had to put her makeup on, select the proper attire, and look perfect before we could leave. When she was ready to go, Jackson would get the car and drive us to the club. As soon as we reached the doorman at the entrance of the club, we were treated like royalty. We would first go to the lounge while the staff was getting our table ready downstairs. The entire staff would greet and fawn over us; it was always "What can we get you, Mrs. Podell?" Mother usually had a cognac and I would have a soda. We would sit in the lounge until my father came out from the kitchen or his office and take us to our table downstairs.

We always sat at the same table, reserved for my father, when we went to the Copa, whether it was a Sunday night or a special occasion. I think Sunday night was chosen as our night to visit the club since it was probably the least busy night of the week. I would be all dolled up in my little white gloves and dress, and people would constantly come over and say hello. My father would always introduce us, but I would be bored to death waiting for the show to start. Sunday night was the most I ever saw of my father all week. He would sit down with us for fifteen or twenty minutes and talk to both of us. It was hard to discuss anything with him because his mind was preoccupied with what was happening at the club. I don't believe he really enjoyed being with us; it was like we were a distraction. He would have a scotch or two and then,

My parents on a golf outing with two friends.

once the show began, he left us. Once in a while, on a rare occasion, he would eat dinner and watch the show with us.

My mother and I performed this ritual from the time I was four years old until I was about sixteen. I saw hundreds of shows and entertainers, so after a while it was no big deal. You name the celebrity and we saw him or her because every Sunday night we had to go to the Copa. Frankie Laine, Johnny Ray, Billy Eckstine, Eddie Fisher, Paul Anka, Martha Raye, Tony Bennett, etc. . . . there weren't too many we missed. My mother still went even after I had stopped going. Mother loved the attention she received as Mrs. Jules Podell and being seen in the club with various celebrities; it was all very glamorous. Her favorite performers were Frank Sinatra and Nat King Cole; she also enjoyed Dean Martin, Tony Bennett, and Jimmy Durante.

In 1947, *Copacabana,* a movie that starred Groucho Marx and Carmen Miranda, was released. The comedic plot involved Groucho as agent Lionel Q. Deveraux, who represents only one client, Carmen Novarro, played by Miranda. Lionel gets Carmen to perform at a club called the Copacabana, as both a Brazilian and a French singer, which is the basis for the comedic situations in the film. Several well-known newspaper columnists of the day, such as Earl Wilson and Louis Sobol, had cameos in the motion picture. Incidentally, Monte Proser would be credited as a producer on the film. That would be one of the last times Proser's name would significantly be linked with the Copacabana.

Carmen Miranda headlined the Copacabana in April 1947, several months before the movie was set to premiere in New York, as a marketing ploy to promote the film. Miranda included songs from the movie as part of her nightclub act. The movie did respectable business

My father playing the vibes while sitting in with the band.

during the first few weeks of its release but was not what you would call a blockbuster in terms of ticket sales, and today it has all but been forgotten.

At the same time, radio host Jack Eigen began broadcasting live from the lounge at the Copa. Eigen would interview celebrities nightly, usually from 1 to 4 A.M. on WINS. This exposure would serve to enhance the Copacabana's image as the most famous nightspot in all of New York. The lounge at the Copa was advertised with the slogan "The Later the Greater, Now There's a Late Show in the Copa Lounge." The official Copa handbill described the scene in the lounge as follows: "All through the night you'll delight in the fabulous food and drink, the bright words and music, served up in the town's favorite meetin' house, the Copa lounge. But along about ten-ish, the place really starts jumping as the famous stay-outs drop in with their pin-ups. The fun starts with a great show, featuring many of the stars from the Copa's current production, but with so much talent in the audience, it usually winds up as a wonderful surprise party. And you're invited!"

Rip Taylor recalls the lounge scene at the Copa: "The most fun place to be was the upstairs lounge between shows. The lounge had a trio of musicians playing and the headliners and comics would get up and perform in between shows. Bobby Darin loved hanging out in the lounge, and if a fight broke out, Bobby would try and calm everyone down; it was hysterical. The lounge was packed every night before and after the shows."

According to record executive Danny Kessler, "The lounge at the Copa was also good place to go hang out and see friends. There was a trio playing music, and late in the evening Jack Eigen would do a radio broadcast from his booth. Executives from the entertainment world would always be there for social and business reasons; prices for the food and drinks were very reasonable. We were always treated exceptionally well by the staff, and the Copa lounge was just a very fun place to spend an evening out in those days."

The exact details and facts remain unclear, but by 1950 almost all traces of Monte Proser would vanish from the Copacabana. My father was now the one with his name on the awnings, menus, ashtrays, matchbooks, ads, etc. . . . Everything and anything that had to do with the Copa now had to do with Jules Podell. Rumor had it that Frank Costello was unhappy with Proser and decided my father should be the boss without interference from anyone since he was doing such a successful job running the entire operation.

Since I was only five years old in 1950, I never knew or heard about Monte Proser. As far as I knew, my father was in charge of the Copacabana and I never questioned how or why; it was just a fact. My mother once told me that my father owned the club along with Jack Entratter. Jack was a close friend of my father's and our family. My father and Jack started the Jules Podell Foundation together, which exists to this day.

Occasionally, there would be stories in the press about the Copa and that led to classmates at school saying that my father was a gangster. I'd reply, "You're crazy." If I asked my mother she would answer, "Don't be silly, your father is not a gangster. The Copa is a public place and anybody off the street can walk in." Her explanation made sense to me. I once asked her about Frank Costello because his name surfaced in the papers regarding the Copa and my father. Mother just said that Frank Costello was a very nice gentleman. Costello was obviously involved with the Copa and my father, but that had no effect on me. I don't remember Frank but I remember his girlfriend because she baby-sat for me once or twice. Years later, I recall my mother laughing when Frank Costello's name was mentioned on a television show we were watching. I asked her why she was laughing and she said, "Don't you remember so-and-so? She use to babysit you . . . well, she was Mr. Costello's girlfriend." All I could remember was that his girlfriend was very pretty and nice to me as a child.

The only other time I ever heard my mother mention so-called gangsters was when she said that the biggest gentlemen in the whole world are "connected." My mother told me, "You know, those Mob guys, they really know how to treat a lady, and the biggest gentleman I ever met was Frank Costello." She also added that Nat King Cole was a real gentleman to her whenever they met, although Nat Cole obviously was not connected to the same element as Frank Costello)

The 1950s would be a very good decade for the Copacabana, but things didn't start off that well. During April 1950, Frank Sinatra was playing an engagement at the club, and while his popularity had recently declined, he still was a huge draw at the Copa. On Wednesday, April 26, Sinatra was unable to sing because he suffered a throat hemorrhage at the start of his performance. Singer Billy Eckstine subbed for Sinatra, who was forced to cancel the remaining shows of his engagement.

In 1952, Jack Entratter, who was now listed as the general manager of the Copa, among other things, packed up his family and headed to Las Vegas. Entratter was summoned and asked to be the entertainment director of a new hotel casino in the desert city—the Sands. It was an offer he could not refuse. The powers that be behind the Sands had also enlisted Jackie Friedman of Texas to front as the president of the new venture. I was told that Dad bought out Jack's share of the Copa and thus became the sole owner of the club.

Entratter had established relationships with many of the stars who had played the Copa through the years and enlisted them to join the roster of entertainment headliners at the new Sands Hotel and Casino. Jack, with permission, even named the showroom the Copa Room, and put together his own group of Copa Girls. There were no problems between the Copa in New York and the Sands since the hotel casino was a joint enterprise run by the Genovese family and the Chicago Outfit. You could say it was all in the family, so to speak.

"I left the Copa and New York in 1952, the same time that Jack Entratter left. Jack asked me and a few other girls in the line to move to Las Vegas and open the Copa Room at the Sands. I did move to Las Vegas and worked at the Sands as a Copa girl, but it was different. Las Vegas back then was really a small town and not very sophisticated, worlds apart from New York. If you were a Copa Girl in New York, it was prestigious; people would approach us for an autograph because we were the best there was. Being a Copa Girl in New York City, you really felt like you were somebody special and it was an honor. Being a Copa Girl in Las Vegas was an honor but did not have the same cachet," says Lynn Kessler.

In 1953, Frank Sinatra became the main attraction at the Sands in Las Vegas once his contract at the Desert Inn had expired. Sinatra was happy to join his friend Jack Entratter and perform at the new hotel casino. Together, Entratter and Sinatra would turn the Sands into the number one hotel on the Las Vegas strip—the one place in town where everyone wanted to stay and play whenever they visited the city. Today, Jack Entratter is considered one of the greatest entertainment directors in the history of Las Vegas. Entratter's knowledge, personality, connections, and hard work helped turn Las Vegas into the entertainment capital of the world.

The Sands remained the crown jewel in Las Vegas for several decades until Howard Hughes came to town on a buying spree. In 1996, the Sands was imploded to make room for the Venetian Hotel. Although the structure is long gone, the Sands will forever be synonymous with Las Vegas and the city's golden era before corporations took over the town and megaresorts sprang up.

I remember being sad when Jack Entratter and his family moved west since they were always over at our house for holidays and parties. During those times, I would play with his daughters and liked them very much. I really loved Jack's wife, Dorothy; she was a free spirit. She was blonde and beautiful; she looked like she could have been a Copa girl. Dorothy was the closest thing to a friend my mom ever had besides Ethyl Som. I remember my mother being in shock when Dorothy told her she'd had a boob job. She couldn't believe it, and Dorothy put my mother's hand on her breast to feel it. Breast implants were rare back then.

The Copa Girls

Besides its standing among top nightclubs, the Copa was also becoming known as the place for casting agents and movie producers to find new talent. In 1947, the now long-defunct *Pageant* magazine did a profile on this very subject.

> In the past six years a New York nightclub called the Copacabana has attained a unique position in the entertainment world. Highly successful in its own right, it also has come to be regarded as one

Legendary nightclub entertainer Jimmy Durante holds court at the club after one of his performances.

of the nation's top showcases for potential Hollywood talent.

Among "Copa" dancers, singers, and other performers to hit the celluloid trail are crooner Perry Como, hoofer June Allyson (now the pride of MGM), comedian Jimmy Durante (who began a sensational comeback at the Copa). Others include many a name that the public knows, or will know. Talent scouts, producers, executives follow Copa shows as they follow no other nightclub in the U.S.

Obviously, this is not deliberate Copa policy. Rather, it is the result of a singularly successful approach to entertaining the average nightspot customer. Where most clubs focus on socialites or Broadwayites or tourists, the Copa cuts across the board. Faintly Latin American in decor and atmosphere, it bases its appeal on good food and liquor, excellent dance music (by two orchestras) and a lavish floorshow.

My cousin, Jackie, dressed as a waiter and flanked by the world famous Copa Girls.

The show is the crux of the matter. Changed four times a year, it is produced with the care and glitter of a Broadway revue. Costumes alone cost up to $30,000. Each show has a special musical score (typical recent hits: "No Can Do," "The Coffee Song"). Headlined performers draw headline-worthy salaries: comedian Joe E. Lewis, $5,000 a week; singer Tony Martin, $6,500. Show girls receive $100 a week the year-round-highest regular rate in the country.

The Copa is the only New York night spot to put on three shows a night, seven nights a week. Its late (2:00 am) performance has become a rendezvous for talent around town. Often customers are entertained, impromptu by such "name" guests as Frank Sinatra, Orson Welles, Dinah Shore.

Net result: in a room seating 650, the Copa averages more than 7,500 customers a week, a weekly take of more than $50,000.

Some speculate that even more than the headliners, the main attraction at the nightclub was the Copa Girls. Originally billed as the "Copa Babies" or "Samba Sirens," the Copa Girls would become world famous. The Copa Girls were regarded as the most beautiful showgirls in all of New York. In the first few years of the club's existence, the girls would be introduced to the audience by their own theme song, "You Just Can't Copa with a Copacabana Baby."

In addition to beauty, the major requirement was a girl's ability to dance any number that was incorporated into the current Copa revue. Normally, the average age of the girls was twenty years old. Youth was a prerequisite, since the girls had to perform a total of twenty-one shows per week. The girls did not have much time in between shows to do anything except to grab a bite to eat. Rehearsals for the revues would usually take four to six weeks before it would debut in front of a paying crowd.

In 1942, eighteen of the twenty-five girls who worked as Copa Girls signed a contract with a Hollywood agent or went into a Broadway musical.

"Jack Entratter hired me and we auditioned for an entire week, starting on Monday, before he made his decision on Friday. As a Copa Girl, we had to be at the club by 6:30 P.M. and didn't get finished until

Copa Girls Shirley Cutler, far left bottom, and Lynn Shannon with entertainer Jimmy Durante.

3 A.M. or so; we did three shows a night back then. The shows began at 8 and we would do an opening, middle, and closing number for each show. There was one big dressing room and each girl had her own mirror and dressing table, but it was small area. Doug Coudy was the chorographer and he would walk into our dressing room at any time—even when we would be getting dressed; he was the first gay man I ever knew. As far as the pay was concerned, back then, in the early 1950s, we got $125 a week, which was great money," says former Copa Girl Lynn Kessler.

My father was proud of the Copa Girls and over the years did all he could to help mold and enhance their image. Doug Coudy, who was originally hired as a choreographer at the club, looked after the girls and was a mentor to many of them. Coudy, more than anyone else, worked with the girls to help perfect their enduring style. The public-relations man for the club—I believe it was Sy Preston—would boast in a 1960 release, "The Copa Girls caused a delightful revolution in show business. For generations showgirls had been dressed in fantastic scaffoldings of feathers and plumes, or else in silly satin suits like drum majorettes. The Copa Girls began by being the most exciting models in America's greatest city for beautiful models, and then—they were dressed in the very height of Paris and New York fashion. The Copa Girls are not only the World's Most Beautiful; they are also the World's Most Stylish Girls. At the last count, forty-four Copa Girls have gone to Hollywood from the Copa floor. Among the famous names you know who were Copa Girls are Martha Stewart, Lucille Bremer, June Allyson, Olga San Juan, Janice Rule. . ."

When I was at the club, especially as a child, I would sneak back to the Copa Girls' dressing room and talk with them; they were always very friendly to me. I remember how exciting it was to see them all made up and in their costumes, which were amazing. I could never figure out how they were able to be so poised while wearing their large headdresses and high heels. The Copa Girls were all gorgeous; every girl back then dreamed of being one. Their dressing rooms were narrow and full of large mirrors. Their job was difficult because they were on and off the stage due to numerous costume changes required during a show. I never saw the girls mingling with the customers while I was at the club; I believe my father had a strict rule about that. I recall that the comedian Jan Murray met his wife while she was a Copa Girl. I didn't see my father interact much around the Copa Girls; I think he would talk to Doug Coudy if he wanted something changed or altered in their act. In all the years of shows I never saw the girls make one mistake; they were always perfect.

Nat King Cole, Roy Campanella, and my father pose for this photo with the Copa Girls. Campanella, a catcher for the Brooklyn Dodgers, was paralyzed in a 1958 auto accident.

The Copa Kitchen

My father was a detail-oriented boss and a perfectionist. He was hands-on regarding all aspects and operations involved with the Copa, especially in the kitchens. Above all, he prided himself on the cuisine at the club. In fact, he was so proud of the food that he considered himself as restaurateur instead of nightclub owner. The following would be printed on the Copa handbills:

> The Copa cuisine and the Copa kitchens are under the personal supervision of Jule Podell. The Copa is known as the one nightclub in New York City where the old phrase "night club food" does not apply. Smart New Yorkers are aware that the Copa's food is equal of that served at the top eating places of this food-conscious town. We wish that we could take every one of you on a tour of these truly fabulous kitchens where the Copa food is prepared. They are huge, exciting, filled with food and drink of the finest quality, and all prepared by master chefs. The astonishing thing about the Copa is that it costs less to eat here than in most of New York's fine restaurants—and the show, the dancing, the beautiful girls, the atmosphere, the excitement, is not even added to your check. It adds up to the smartest entertainment buy in New York.

Unless you were a waiter, captain, chef, or entertainer—not many were allowed to enter the sanctuary of the Copa kitchens, which my father ruled with an iron fist.

My father also had a kitchen dedicated to Chinese cuisine. "The Copa is famous in New York for its Oriental dishes, and there's a good reason why. We maintain a separate Chinese unit in our kitchens, staffed by the finest native chefs. If you are a lover of Chinese food you

The captains and waiters in the Copa kitchen preparing for the evening dinner crowd.

will agree with those who have said that there is no better Chinese food served anywhere!"

Dad was also pleased that not only the customers but the press raved about the food at the Copa. Columnist Martin Burden wrote in the *New York Post*, "When you visit the Copa you're in for a treat. It's a great buy, a comparatively inexpensive way to sample the best nightlife our city has to offer, and the Copa kitchens turn out some of the best food in town." And New York columnist Robert W. Dana filed this review on June 13, 1949 headlined FOOD IS TOPS, TOO, AT THE COPACABANA:

> In all the years it has gained a nationwide reputation for its excellent shows, fine music and gilt-edged atmosphere, the Copacabana, 10 E. 60th St., has been doing an outstanding job of preparing food in immaculate kitchens behind the scenes. So often I have heard the remark: "We never knew a night club could serve such food" that I decided to meet the chefs.
>
> That entails too much meeting during the busy dinner hour, what with 20 chefs and cooks in all—15 preparing a French cuisine and five a list of Chinese dishes. So it was restricted to a fast handshake with Marcel Jougier, head French chef, who has been there six years, and a nod to Lum On, head Chinese chef.
>
> The rest of the time was devoted to watching Jules Podell, the club's supervising director and a restaurant man for 30 years, watching each waiter like a hawk to make sure that each order is as near perfection as possible. Down the line they came, bearing their trays of edibles. Quickly the stocky man in the brown suit lifted each cover, made sure the size of the portion and the general appearance of the plate was right, otherwise back the waiter went to the back of the line to try all over again.

Mania for Cleanliness

You'd think that running the one gauntlet would suffice, but, no, the waiter has to satisfy the head checker before leaving the kitchen for the final trip to the customer. Mr. Podell has a mania on the subject of cleanliness. Let him see a piece of lettuce staining the floor and he'll stop everything to have it cleaned up. Let a waiter show a spot on his white jacket with the crimson collar and a quick change is ordered.

Out front, Jack Entratter, the quietly efficient manager, watches the customers' satisfaction, exemplified, perhaps in a group of women having a dinner party on the balcony.

They not only are going to see one of the town's best night club shows, but they're going to eat a tasty, filling table d'hôte dinner, with entrees ranging in price from $2.50 for filet of lemon sole Breteuil to $4.25 for roast stuffed Vermont tom turkey. Some of the other fishes are scaloppini of veal (always excellent), emince of capon with spaghetti Tetrazzinni, baby lamb steak béarnaise and such Chinese dishes as white meat chicken chow mein and pepper steak with bamboo shoots, water chestnuts, mushrooms and fresh tomatoes.

Menu Memos: Copacabana, 10 E. 60th St. Excellent French and Chinese cuisines. Joe Lopez, headwaiter, Table d'hote dinners served from 7 to 10 p.m., $2.50 to $6.50 for filet mignon. Also an extensive à la carte list. Current floor show stars Dean Martin and Jerry Lewis, the fine comedy team, in their seventh week. Mary Raye and Naldi, the dancers, have just joined the show as featured performers, with the Copa girls youthful singers and dancers comprising the rest of the entertainment.

My father, Mack Gray, Dick Stabile, Dean Martin, and Jerry Lewis pose with the chefs in the kitchen. Gray worked for Dean while Stabile was the musical director for Martin and Lewis.

Prom Season

One of the highlights every year was prom season at the Copa. It soon became a tradition; the hip place to go after your school prom was the Copa. Teenagers would line the streets in order to make sure they could get a table for their special night. The way to impress any girl on a date was to take her to the Copa after the prom. One evening during prom season I stopped by the club—of course the lines were around the block—to see my father. I obviously did not have on a prom dress and was not there with a date; I was by myself. I usually knew the bouncer at the front door, but this night it was a new person, and he stopped me as I was heading into the club. I explained to him that I was not crashing the line and was not there as part of any prom group. He said, "No, go to the end of the line like everyone else." I said, "Excuse me, my father is Mr. Podell." So he looked at me, laughed, and said, "Sure he is." Now, you can imagine, the kids in line started heckling me and told me to get in line like everyone else. I finally told the doorman to go ask Raymond, the captain, to come to the front door and verify that I was Mr. Podell's daughter. After a few minutes, Raymond appeared and set the man straight. That night, my father fired the bouncer. Afterward, I felt bad about the entire incident and would always use the back entrance of the club to avoid something like this happening again.

In the early 1960s, Chubby Checker released a song called "The Twist" and the single along with the dance became a hit with teenagers around the country. Around this time I was planning my prom party and my father said, "It's your prom and you can have anyone you want to perform," so I said, "I want Chubby Checker." Dad looked puzzled, as Chubby had never appeared at the Copa, and he had never even

Another shot taken outside the club during prom season.

heard of him or the twist. I dragged my mother to the Peppermint Lounge to see Chubby's act. Mom enjoyed the show and told Dad, who, in turn, contacted Chubby's people to let him know I had requested him to perform for my prom party. This would be the first of Chubby's many appearances at the Copa. It was a very exciting night and the prom kids loved his show; I'm not sure it was Father's cup of tea, but he saw the crowd reaction and hired Chubby to work again at the Copa many more times as a headliner.

Comedian Rip Taylor said, "I was booked during prom season several times at the Copa and I would change my act because there were high school kids in the audience. Not that I worked dirty but I would tailor the jokes for the students. One night I told a joke about an Indian that drinks too much tea and the punch line was 'he gets caught in his tea pee.' I heard Mr. Podell tap his ring on the table after that

A group of high school seniors, after their prom, inside the Copa attending a performance by Paul Anka. Anka was a huge draw, especially, for the younger set.

line. Once I finished my act, Mr. Podell flew back and said, 'I don't want no filth in the Copa.' I explained that it was an innocent play on words, but he insisted it was risqué and filthy and not appropriate for his club. Jules Podell was very meticulous about clean material and naturally I obeyed him. I still don't think the line is dirty!"

"As a performer, be it a singer, dancer, comic, musician, you name it, working at the Copacabana was the pinnacle of everyone's desire as a star—there's no doubt about it. The Copa was glamorous, had great entertainment and was a wonderful place to spend an evening. The food was also excellent because Jules Podell supervised everything that went on in the kitchen; that is where he spent most of his time each night. I don't believe anyone ever complained about the food or service at the club. I look back on my days at the Copa and it was the happiest and most exciting time of my life. The celebrities I met and worked with were wonderful and I met my husband, Danny, there . . . it was a great time!" says Lynn Kessler.

CHAPTER 3

Martin and Lewis and Friends

My father's inner sanctum consisted of Frank Sinatra, Dean Martin, Jerry Lewis, Sammy Davis Jr., Joe E. Lewis, and Jimmy Durante, mainly because they were the big money-makers for the club. Many celebrities would come to our house over the years; they would wait for my father and then go behind closed doors in his den.

Dean Martin came together with Jerry Lewis, or they would come over separately. My father liked Dean better than Jerry; Jerry could be loud and obnoxious. I didn't think Jerry was funny; I thought he was mean and didn't really like kids. Dean, on the other hand, was always nice to me and I had a crush on him because he was so handsome. My father got

An ad for one of the many appearances at the Copacabana by Dean Martin and Jerry Lewis. Without question, the duo was one of the most popular comedy teams of all time.

along with most of the entertainers who played the Copa through the years. Frank Sinatra, I would have to say, was his favorite singer and performer. I remember Sinatra as more of a man's man; when he came to our house he would talk mostly with my dad about business or they told jokes to each other. Jimmy Durante and Joe E. Lewis were probably my father's best show-business friends; they were the ones who came over to the house the most often. I don't think my father ever socialized with anyone who was not in one way or another associated with the Copacabana.

The "Rat Pack" consisted of Frank Sinatra, Dean Martin, Sammy Davis Jr., Joey Bishop, and Peter Lawford. The Rat Pack never appeared together as a group onstage at the Copacabana, as they did at the Sands Copa Room in Las Vegas. However, each performer did, at various times, play the Copa. Sinatra, Martin, and Davis eclipsed both Bishop and Lawford and were top attractions whenever they played the club.

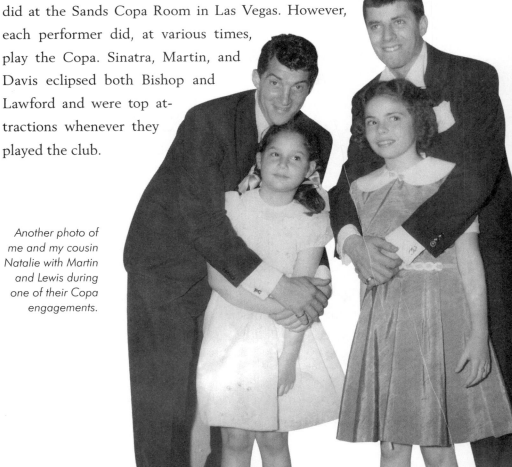

Another photo of me and my cousin Natalie with Martin and Lewis during one of their Copa engagements.

Me with my cousins, Jackie and Natalie, pose for a photo with Dean and Jerry in the Copa kitchen with my mother.

Peter Lawford and my father pose with a chef in the Copa kitchen. Besides being a movie star, Lawford would also attempt a career as a nightclub performer; it was short lived.

Me, Peter Lawford, and my friend, Tobey Holzer, pose for a photo in the Copa kitchen.

Sammy Davis Jr., Dad, and Dean Martin. My father liked both Sammy and Dean, as performers and friends.

Dean Martin and Jerry Lewis

Next to Sinatra, the most famous act to play the Copa was Dean Martin and Jerry Lewis. Today, it is hard to imagine the meteoric rise and popularity of this comedy team. At the time, Laurel and Hardy were all but forgotten, and Abbott and Costello were coasting on their earlier fame. Martin and Lewis filled the void and captured the public's fancy, becoming successful on radio, television, and movies and through personal appearances.

It would be two years after they joined forces that Martin and Lewis would play the Copacabana. Their agent, Abby Greshler, had pitched the duo to Jack Entratter previously and he passed on them, but in 1948 he decided to give them a shot at the club. At first, Martin and Lewis balked, as they would be taking a pay cut and backseat—

Dean Martin and Jerry Lewis do one of their zany comedy routines with their musical director Dick Stabile at the club.

Dean Martin waiting to catch an object being thrown by Jerry Lewis as Dick Stabile cracks up over the duo's antics.

opening for the star attraction Vivian Blaine. Abby Greshler convinced Martin and Lewis that if they were a hit at the Copacabana they would be on the road to superstardom. That was all it took—aside from Greshler threatening to quit as their manager—and the comedy team signed to play to Copa for a two-week engagement beginning on April 8, 1948.

What happened on their opening night at the Copacabana was so surreal it now sounds as if it were scripted. Martin and Lewis were such a smash with the Copa audience that poor Vivian Blaine literally left the stage in tears after the audience kept calling for more of the duo during her act. In between shows, my father informed Martin and Lewis that he was going to make some changes with the billing; they would now be the headliners. When Ms. Blaine was told of the new billing, she abruptly quit, leaving Martin and Lewis as the headline act for the rest of the scheduled engagement.

Variety summed it up best in their review: "Dean Martin and Jerry Lewis really hit the big-time at their opening last Thursday at the Copa. Both have been around singly and jointly, recently at the Capitol on Broadway, but not until their Copa bow did they truly arrive as potential comedy stars."

Along with radio and print praise, such was the word of mouth and positive buzz on their act that my father extended Martin and Lewis's two-week engagement to six weeks; he also raised their salary to $5,000 a week. But even that wasn't enough—Dad would keep extending their engagement until they eventually closed eighteen weeks after they first opened. Perhaps the most important patron seeing Martin and Lewis during their run at the Copa was movie producer Hal Wallis. Wallis was so impressed with the comedy team that he eventually signed

1444

My father with Jerry Lewis, Jimmy Durante, and Dean Martin getting ready to cut a
cake that had an image of Durante drawn on it.

them to a production deal with Paramount Pictures and would help turn the duo into bona fide movie stars.

Martin and Lewis would play the Copacabana many times during the next eight years and both became friends and guests of Jules Podell at his home. Thus, it was only fitting that when they decided to end their career together as a team, it would be at the Copacabana, the venue where they were first catapulted into superstardom. Their July 1956 engagement was the hottest ticket in town—if not the world. According to Arthur Marx, who recounted the following in his book *Everybody Loves Somebody Sometime*:

> Although Dean and Jerry had never been funnier, the bitterness of the impending divorce was apparent. During a roughhouse clowning routine at the chic bistro one night, Dean brought his left heel down on Jerry's foot with the force of a pile driver. Jerry let out a shriek that could be heard as far as Staten Island. Dean claimed absolutely no vindictiveness involved. "It was only an accident," he told reporters. This infighting, however, didn't prevent them from putting on a "schmaltzy" closing night performance, climaxed by their singing "Pardners" (from their next-to-last picture together) and embracing and kissing affectionately for the benefit of all their misty-eyed well-wishers who were urging them to stay together. But once the phony sentimentality of the occasion had faded away into the past along with the cigarette smoke and the body odor of the prancing Copa Girls, Jerry was suddenly overcome with grave doubts about his ability to face the future without Dean.

Jerry Lewis would later tell *Look* magazine about that last night at the Copacabana: "When we finished the last show together, I went back to my dressing room. I was numb with fright and shaking all over,

my clothes were drenched with perspiration. I sat in my dressing room, crying. I thought I'd never be able to get up before an audience again. I thought it would be impossible for me to work without Dean. After I finished crying in my dressing room, I phoned Patti in California. I said to her, 'It's all over.' She said, 'Don't be afraid. I'm your friend'—and I cracked up completely. Then Dean came in and we both cried. We shook hands and wished each other luck."

Over the years, differing accounts have surfaced about the last night Martin and Lewis worked together at the Copacabana. There is no doubt that Jerry Lewis was sad and somber about the duo's split. Martin, on the other hand, was said to be relieved that this phase of his career had come to an end.

Jules Podell, along with most of the American public, was also unhappy about the comedic duo's breakup. Although he was enjoying the riches of doing record-breaking business during Martin and Lewis's last run, he also knew he would never see their likes again and that meant

My father with Jerry Lewis. Lewis would never play the Copacabana as a solo act after he and Dean Martin broke up their partnership.

My father and a friend look on as Jerry Lewis plays with a book of matches.

he might never see such crowds attempt to shoehorn themselves into the Copa to get a glimpse of the comedy team.

Decades later, after my father had passed away, Jerry would recount a story that supposedly happened soon after the Martin and Lewis breakup. Jerry claimed that my father sent a "tough guy" to his home in Bel Air, California. Podell's messenger suggested to Jerry that he agree to an engagement at the Copa as a solo act or harm might come to him and his family. After the man left, Jerry responded by calling Chicago Mob boss Tony Accardo and explained the situation and Podell's threat. Accardo told Jerry to "forget about it" and not to worry, that he would take care of the situation. According to Jerry, that was the last he ever heard from Jules Podell. Since all the principals except Jerry were deceased when he began telling this story, it is impossible to confirm its validity. P.S., Jerry never played the Copa as a solo act.

Frank Sinatra

The greatest singer of the twentieth century, Frank Sinatra played the most famous nightclub of that century throughout the late 1940s and 1950s. The Copa was the premier nightclub/"saloon" in New York, and there was no other entertainer who was more identified as a saloon singer than Frank Sinatra. In fact, Sinatra embraced the title so much so that his passport stated his occupation as "saloon singer."

Sinatra enjoyed SRO crowds, and his performances at the Copacabana are legendary. The Copa was also home to some low points during the singer's storied career.

Frank Sinatra onstage at the Copacabana wearing a coonskin cap. Sinatra was without question, the most famous singer/entertainer of the 20th century.

The first time Frank Sinatra played the Copa, it was not even his own engagement. On September 9, 1946, Sinatra flew from Los Angeles to New York for Phil Silvers's opening night at the Copacabana. *Look* magazine detailed the story as follows:

> When Silvers was making his first attempt to establish a foothold in the show business big-time, he got a booking to do an act at the Copacabana in New York with the great burlesque comedian Rags Ragland. The two comics went to Hollywood to rehearse. They both knew Sinatra, who offered to help them work out their act. Suddenly, Ragland became ill and died of pneumonia in a Los Angeles hospital; Silvers was devastated. He felt he couldn't do the act alone—that he was finished in show business. He continued to rehearse, however, and flew back to New York for his Copacabana booking.
>
> On opening night, Silvers was brooding in his dressing room when the door burst open and in walked Sinatra. He had gone AWOL from the set of the movie he was making in Hollywood, and had flown to New York. "I'm going to do Rags's part with you tonight," he announced. He did, and it was one of the most exciting and sentimental openings ever seen in New York. From the stimulation he received from that audience, Silvers was able to continue the show alone.

Sinatra would again grace the Copa stage in March 1950; it was to be his first New York nightclub engagement in over four years. At that time, the press was relentless in reporting his every move since he was involved with screen goddess Ava Gardner. No other couple, except, later, perhaps Richard Burton and Liz Taylor, was so dogged by the press. Today, the only comparison might be Brad Pitt and Angelina Jolie. In April 1950, Sinatra was forced to cancel his final two nights at the Copa as he suffered a vocal cord hemorrhage.

Sinatra recalled that night: "I was doing three shows a night at the Copacabana in New York and five days a week on a Lucky Strike radio program, live every night with Dorothy Kirsten. And I was rehearsing every day for something—benefits, concerts, etc. . . . I had a real bad cold and was run down physically—my resistance was knocked out. I came on stage at the Copa one morning about two-thirty A.M. to do the third show. I opened my mouth, and nothing came out—absolutely nothing—just dust. I was never so panic-stricken in my whole life. I remember looking at the audience, a blizzard outside, about seventy people in the place, and they knew something serious had happened. There was absolute silence; stunning, absolute silence. I looked at them, and they looked at me, and I looked at Skitch Henderson, who was playing the piano. His face was ghastly white. Finally, I turned to the audience and whispered into the microphone, 'Good night,' and walked off the floor. It turned out I had a vocal hemorrhage; bleeding in my throat."

In 2004, Skitch Henderson recalled working with Sinatra at the Copacabana in 1950. "Late nights at the Copa I'll remember forever," he said. "He did all the standards, Cole Porter, Rodgers, Gershwin, I've never heard anybody sing lyrics like that. It was never boring. It was fresh every night."

On September 21, 1950, Sinatra recorded the song "Meet Me at the Copa," written by Alex Stordahl, Sinatra's longtime arranger and musical director, and songwriter Sammy Cahn. The song, according to Cahn, was written for Sinatra to sing specifically at the Copacabana during his engagement, as a favor for longtime friend Jack Entratter, the general manager of the club. The lyrics to the song included the line "the most amazing club in town you will admit . . . it's the spot where

Dean Martin, Jerry Lewis, and Frank Sinatra strike a pose at the Copa in 1948. This photo was taken during Martin and Lewis's first engagement at the club.

stars come just to see the stars." However, unless you attended the Copa during Sinatra's run back then, chances are you would have never heard the song. Columbia Records, Sinatra's label at the time, did not release the recording until several decades later.

Sinatra returned to the Copa in December 1954 for another sold-out engagement, which ran into early 1955. Not only was his singing making headlines, so were his dating habits. Columnist Earl Wilson wrote about Sinatra's relationship with socialite Gloria Vanderbilt: "They had a date that night, December 22, 1954, when he opened at the Copacabana. He sat at her table before his turn and when he sang, she removed her glasses to watch." Another columnist, Dorothy Kilgallen, reported that Sinatra had also invited actress Anita Ekberg to New York for his opening at the Copa: "As the fatal hour approached Frankie drove Julie Podell (owner of the place) close to madness, making sure that Anita had a table ringside, where he could see her and sing his most melting ballads straight at her. This was arranged, but amid considerable backstage turmoil, because nerves are taut on an opening night and this was a big one. Right on cue, just before the show started, the magnificent Anita entered. The predictable number of heads turned and the natural buzz was heard." Joey Bishop, who would later become a member of the famed Rat Pack, was the comedian on the bill with Sinatra during this engagement.

At the same time, Sinatra's earlier employer, Tommy Dorsey, was also in New York. Dorsey was celebrating his twentieth anniversary along with Martin Block, a New York disc jockey. On February 3, 1955, Sinatra stopped by to see Dorsey and was coaxed into singing a few songs with the band. The reunion was broadcast on the radio, with Sinatra mentioning that he couldn't stay too long since "I gotta go to work in a few minutes . . . I'm glad I was in the East to attend." After Sinatra did three songs—"I'll Never Smile Again," "Oh, Look at Me Now," and "This Love of Mine"—the crowd cheered for more. Sinatra took his leave, explaining, "I gotta run away, I wish I had more time to stay around and sing some songs, but Jules Podell will send out his bull-dogs after me or he'll send himself."

Of that evening Sinatra's longtime pianist, Bill Miller, recalled the following, "Before we did the first show at the Copa . . . Frank said to me, 'I should really do something with Tommy again.' I said that sounds great since I had also worked with Tommy years before for a short time. At this stage of his career, Sinatra had eclipsed Dorsey in terms of popularity, as the big band era was drawing to a close. True to his word, Sinatra arranged for the Dorsey brothers, Tommy and Jimmy, to open his stage show at the Paramount Theatre the following year during the premier run of his current film *Johnny Concho.*

In December 1956 Sinatra opened another engagement at the Copa and *Look* magazine stated:

> In night clubs, Sinatra is now the undisputed King. In no other field is his popularity more apparent. At the Copacabana, a four-abreast line of customers stood in below-freezing cold outside the club each night just to reach the front door with their confirmed reservations. The line extended a hundred yards around the corner. Nearly every evening, there were fist fights among the more impetuous patrons, and in the line, waiting like the rest, were such celebrities as Joe DiMaggio, Gov. William G. Stratton of Illinois and a sable-clad Doris Duke. Inside the club, while Sinatra performed, customers stood on chairs, tables and suitcases. The crowds at the Copacabana were mostly mature people; the hardened, experienced night-club goers who demand "class" in

their entertainment. There was, however, a good sprinkling of young matrons in their late twenties and early thirties who occasionally emitted once-familiar cries of "Oh, Frankie!" when their hero essayed an old-time glissando.

During this engagement, Sinatra's close friend and movie legend Humphrey Bogart passed away, on January 14, 1957. Sinatra, too distraught to sing that evening, asked friends Jerry Lewis and Sammy Davis Jr. to substitute for him. Longtime Sinatra friend Frank Military recalls that evening: "I was with Frank when he was working the Copa and Humphrey Bogart passed away. Frank, myself, and Hank Sanicola, Sinatra's manager, were in the dressing room before the show at the Hotel Fourteen and the phone rang—whoever was on the other end told Frank that Bogart had died. Frank looked at us and said, 'I can't go on tonight; I can't do a show.' Mind you, the place was jam-packed with all the top people in New York. So then Frank says to me, 'I know Jerry Lewis is in town, call him and see if he can do the show tonight.' So I called Jerry and told him what was happening and he said he'd be happy to help Frank out. Within thirty minutes, Jerry meets me at the Copa and we tell Doug Coudy to make the announcement. Coudy gets on the PA systems and says, 'Ladies and Gentlemen, Frank Sinatra will not be appearing tonight but in his place we have Jerry Lewis.' The place went ballistic, they started booing and hollering; they had no idea why Frank couldn't go on. Jerry goes onstage and says into the microphone, 'Frank, I want to talk to you after the show.' Sammy Davis showed up a little later that evening and performed with Jerry."

Sinatra's last formal engagement at the Copacabana was in late 1957 and ran into the first days of 1958. As usual, it was a triumph. According to Bill Miller, "Frank loved working the Copacabana, as I did.

The Copa was the 'top nightclub' in those days . . . every major singer and comedian was booked there at one time or another./Being in New York with Frank was always exciting and the crowds at the Copa loved him because it was his home turf, so to speak. I think next to Las Vegas and the 500 Club in Atlantic City, the Copa audiences were really Frank's type of people and he always gave them a great show. Jules Podell was a real character, almost like something out of *Guys and Dolls*. Podell was always nice to me and I never heard Frank say a cross word about him; they seemed to get along just fine. Podell was a no-nonsense guy, just like Frank, so they didn't have any problems communicating with one another.")

In November 1960, Sinatra and the Copacabana would briefly make headlines in the New York papers. One headline, in the *Daily News*, read COPA ON THE CARPET: HOW DID SINATRA SING SANS LICENSE? The story centered on a probe involving comic/humorist Richard (Lord) Buckley and his New York cabaret card. New York city commissioner Louis Kaplan "announced late yesterday that he will call in the management of the Copacabana night club and demand records and an explanation why Frank Sinatra performed there in 1957 without first obtaining a performer's permit from the NY Police Department's License Bureau. The commissioner said the investigation will go far beyond a checkup on the Citizens Emergency Committee's charge that an effort was made to extort a $100 bribe from Lord Buckley, who sought restoration of his card after it had been revoked because he had concealed an old arrest record for drunkenness and marijuana possession." The above headlines turned out to be a moot point. Having a New York City Cabaret Identification Card had become a requirement during Prohibition; according to the law, a permit had to be held by all those

Frank Sinatra poses with a group of Peter Som's fraternity brothers backstage at the Copa. Som stands next to Sinatra on his left.

who worked in a New York City nightclub. Although "Lord" Buckley passed away soon after his card was seized, the so-called scandal eventually helped dismantle the antiquated system; Commissioner Kennedy left office and the cabaret-card requirement was abolished within a few months.

Although Frank Sinatra would never appear as a headliner at the Copacabana again, when he was in New York, he would occasionally stop by the club to see other performers and say hello to Jules Podell. My father was also fond of Sinatra, and in November 1965, he placed an ad in *Billboard* magazine, a special issue celebrating Sinatra's fiftieth birthday and twenty-fifth anniversary in the entertainment business, that simply read CONGRATULATIONS, JULES PODELL. Podell would also send Sinatra telegrams before his major openings in Las Vegas wishing him the best of luck.

Sammy Davis Jr.

Because of his vast array of talents—singing, dancing, imitations, etc.—Sammy Davis Jr. was the personification of a consummate nightclub headliner. Sammy first played the Copacabana in 1954, as part of the Will Mastin Trio. Sammy had been working with his father and uncle since he was three years old, but he was without question the star of the group. The Will Mastin Trio, especially Sammy, had longed to play the Copa for many years, as they knew it was the top nightclub in the world.

But the first time Sammy Davis ever set foot in the Copacabana was to see Frank Sinatra. Sammy's initial attempt to see Sinatra at the

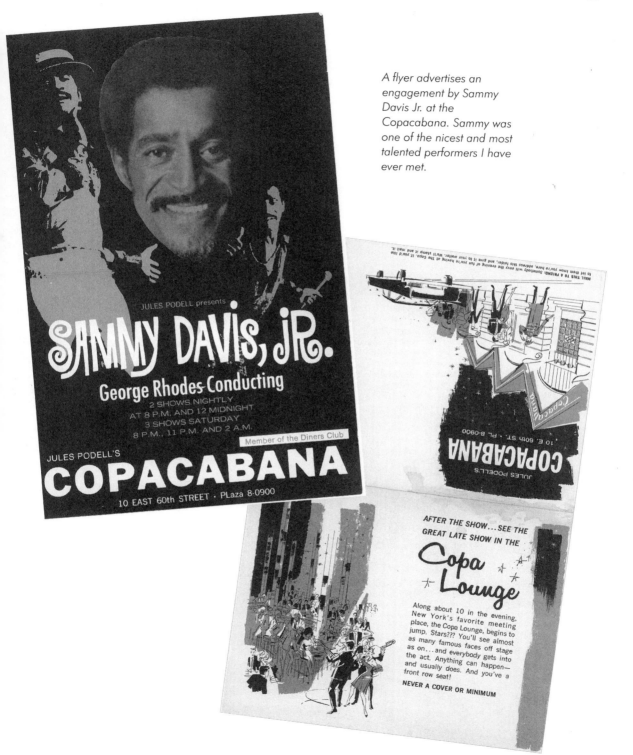

A flyer advertises an engagement by Sammy Davis Jr. at the Copacabana. Sammy was one of the nicest and most talented performers I have ever met.

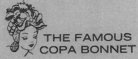

THE FAMOUS COPA BONNET

Only the really great are entitled to wear the Copa's symbol of success. It's the Night Club Academy Award... the Laurel Wreath of Stardom. Just look at the talented stars who have worn the Bonnet:

1. ....Jimmy Durante
2. ....Dean Martin
3. .... Dionne Warwick
4. .... Joe E. Lewis
5. .... Johnny Mathis
6. .... Frank Sinatra
7. ....Danny Thomas
8. ....Tony Bennett
9. .... Peggy Lee
10. ....Steve Lawrence
11. ....Sammy Davis, Jr.
12. ....Joey Bishop
14. .... Diana Ross and
 The Supremes
15. .... Eydie Gorme
16. ....Bobby Darin
17. .... Jerry Lewis
18. .... Jimmy Roselli
19. .... Jerry Vale
20. .... Connie Francis
21. ....Tom Jones
22. .... Paul Anka

THE CAPTIVATING, SCINTILLATING COPA! This is where it pens . . . the glitter of sparkling entertainment . . . the fun and excitement of "a goes". . . the electricity that makes the Copa "The Great American Night Club". Th —inventor of what's best in cafe entertainment, hands you the evening filled with th dance-able music in town . . .the most star-strewn musical revues East of Broadw and a night to remember!

THE GREAT COPA SHOW Where else but the world-famous Copa wou unbelievable talents perform for your entertainment pleasure? No where else— the Copa is the showcase for the stars. The biggest stars can and do call the Cop —stars like those illustrated above—like the one you'll see tonight . . . holders famed Copa bonnet . . . recipients of the world's acclaim. They're all here for you ment. Watch and see for yourself!

inside of flyer

A flyer advertises an engagement by Sammy Davis Jr. at the Copacabana.

UISINE A LA COPA Just marvelous! This is because the Copa has a reputation
ve up to . . . a reputation for the finest in everything. Master chefs whip up outstand-
gourmet menus in kitchens any woman would adore. Service is a happy, courteous
erience. Surprisingly enough, Copa Cuisine will cost you far less than most of our
n's finest restaurants. You'll enjoy the sumptuous cuisine, the show, the dancing, and
excitement without a pinch to your wallet.

INESE FOOD SERVED HERE Oriental cooking is so important to the
a's guests, we have separate kitchens, just to prepare it. Our native chefs keep every-
g authentic and serve up a tantalizing menu of savory Chinese specialties.
Copa Cuisine and Kitchens are personally supervised by Jules Podell.

COPACABANA
MBER OF THE DINERS' CLUB—10 E. 60th STREET, PLaza 8-0900

Copa was not a pleasant one. Podell, like many of that generation, had racist tendencies; at that time it was embedded in the culture and fabric of America. But one man, Frank Sinatra, stood against and fought segregation and racism throughout his life and career. Sammy Davis, until his death, would recount the story of how Sinatra stood firm so his friend could attend his performance at the nightclub. Sinatra had invited Sammy along with drummer Buddy Rich to attend his show. When the doorman saw Sammy in the group, he claimed he could not find their reservation. Sammy and Buddy Rich left in disgust, not wanting to start a commotion. When Sinatra found out about the incident, he was livid. He called Sammy, apologized for the problem, and told him to show up that evening as his guest. Sinatra, true to his character, told Jules Podell and Jack Entratter that Sammy would be his guest and should be treated accordingly. Sinatra also told them both how angry he was and did not want to scream and shout since it could jeopardize his singing voice and that might force him to cancel the engagement. Both Podell and Entratter got Sinatra's message loud and clear. Sinatra, who was at a low point in his career and needed the gig more than the Copacabana needed him, made sure that Sammy was treated with respect and dignity while attending his performance at the Copa, and all else be damned. This was a pivotal moment in the life of Sammy Davis Jr. and also in the life of the Copa. Sinatra was instrumental in breaking the color barrier at the Copa, as he would also be a few years later in Las Vegas.

Sammy would go on to play the Copa as a headliner both with the Will Mastin Trio and as a solo act. His shows were always one of the highlights of the season. Sammy was one of a handful of superstars who continued to play the Copa up until Jules Podell passed away.

Another flyer, at this time, Sammy Davis Jr. was still a member of the Will Mastin Trio. Sammy, a few years later, would leave the group and venture out as a solo act. Sammy signed the back of this flyer to me.

There's a new star over New York

as
JULES PODELL
presents

the Manhattan Cafe Debut of the

WILL MASTIN TRIO

featuring

SAMMY DAVIS, JR.

MARY SMALL
PAGE AND BRAY

BETTY LORRAINE & CHUCK BRUNNER
SANDY EVANS

The World Famous Copa Girls
MICHAEL DURSO and The COPACABANA ORCHESTRA
FRANK MARTI and The COPA SAMBA BAND

Staged by **DOUGLAS COUDY** • Words and Music by **BOB HILLIARD & DAVE MANN**
Orchestrations by **PHIL LANG** • Costumes Designed by **MICHI** • Executed by **MME. BERTHE**
Furs by **PETERZIL & COHEN** • Jewelry by **CORO**
MEMBER OF THE DINERS' CLUB

JULES PODELL'S

COPACABANA

10 EAST 60TH STREET • PLaza 8-0900

NO COVER • NO MINIMUM • NO CABARET TAX

by the biggest little bands in town, usually with a few strings attached,

6 P.M. to closing, along with

Hand-Holdin' Music

Both American and Chinese percussion, is served nightly from

Fabulous Food

you're in the mood for food, for drink, for chit and for chat, make
a bee-line for the Copa Lounge.

the number one place in town for putting hearts together. Anytime

make
THE Copa Lounge

Soft Lights and Sweet Music

We're At
The Copa!
Where Are You?

To "MAHDA
MAY GOD BE WITH YOU
ALWAYS
Sammy Davis

MAIL THIS TO A FRIEND: Somebody will envy the evening of fun you're having at The Copa. If you'd like to let them know you're here, address this folder and give it to your waiter. We'll stamp it and mail it.

• THE COPACABANA
10 E. 60TH ST., NEW YORK, 22

THE Copa TRADITION
the Great American Night Club

As the Copa enters its 'teens, it looks back on a dozen golden years of fabulous, unforgettable nights, nights of laughter, nights of excitement. It's no mystery why the Copa is the most glamorous night club in the big town, for this is New York's heart-quarters for great stars, great stars on the stage and at the tables, for the Copa is the show case of show business. On the Copa floor more stars have been born than in any other night club anytime, anywhere. Add to this the Copa Girls, the Most Beautiful Girls in the World, whose graduates are among the brightest stars in the entertainment world. The Copa is justly proud of its wonderful, high quality food, acknowledged by smart New Yorkers as the equal of that served in the nation's finest restaurants. Add the most exciting dance music in town. Add the electric atmosphere, the exciting sense that something important is happening, and that's the Copa. The real miracle is that all this is brought to you at the most sensible cabaret prices in town. No wonder the Copa is known throughout the world as The Great American Night Club.

the Copa Bonnet

The Copa bonnet is a symbolic award to those stars who have scored memorable successes in our gay Copa revues. It has been called the Night Club Academy Award, the Oscar of after-dark entertainment. Certainly it is one of the most coveted symbols of success in all of the show world, and little wonder, for just take a look at only a few of the greats who have won the Copa bonnet over the years.

THE *Copa* GIRLS

The Copa girls caused a delightful revolution in show business. For generations show girls had been dressed in fantastic scaffoldings of feathers and plumes, or else in silly satin suits like drum majorettes. The Copa Girls began by being the most exciting models in America's greatest city for beautiful models, and then—they were dressed in the very height of Paris and New York fashion. The Copa Girls are not only the World's Most Beautiful, they are also the World's Most Stylish Girls. At the last count, 44 Copa Girls had gone to Hollywood from the Copa Floor. Among the famous names you know who were Copa Girls are Martha Stewart, Lucille Bremer, June Allyson, Olga San Juan . . .

THE *Copa* KITCHENS

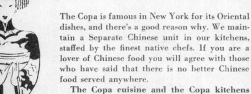

The Copa is known as the one night club in New York City where the old phrase "night club food", does not apply. Smart New Yorkers are aware that the Copa's food is the equal of that served at the top eating places of this food-conscious town. We wish that [c]ould take every one of you on a tour of these truly fabulous kitchens where the Copa food is [prep]ared. They are huge, exciting, filled with food and drink of the finest quality, and all prepared [by m]aster chefs. The astonishing thing about the Copa is that it costs less to eat here than in most [of N]ew York's fine restaurants—and the show, the dancing, the beautiful girls, the atmosphere, the [excit]ement, is not even added to your check. It adds up to the smartest entertainment buy in New York.

THE CHINESE CUISINE

The Copa is famous in New York for its Oriental dishes, and there's a good reason why. We maintain a Separate Chinese unit in our kitchens, staffed by the finest native chefs. If you are a lover of Chinese food you will agree with those who have said that there is no better Chinese food served anywhere.

The Copa cuisine and the Copa kitchens are under the personal supervision of Jules Podell.

inside of flyer

Another flyer, at this time, Sammy Davis, Jr. was still a member of the Will Mastin Trio. Sammy, a few years later, would leave the group and venture out as a solo act. Sammy signed the back of this flyer to me.

Sammy Davis Jr. would become good friends with my father as the years went by. I remember one specific night when Sammy came over to our apartment and my nurse summoned me to my father's den. With trepidation, I made my way to the den and I hid behind my nurse. Sammy had on a long coat, and while he and my father were talking, all of a sudden a whimpering sound and movement came from within Sammy's coat. All I could see peeking out of the coat was this little black nose looking at me as Sammy smiled and opened up his coat to reveal a miniature poodle that was a gift for me. I thought this was the greatest thing in the world, since my father had never allowed an animal in the house. He didn't want the dog, but my mother said it was a gift, so we got to keep him; I named the dog Tinker.

We never had a pet because my father had a phobia against animals being in the house. Both my mother and I loved animals; I favored cats. Also, living in a high-rise was not conducive to proper exercise and walks. I have seen pictures of me, when I was two or three years old, on vacation in Florida playing with a kitten. I think my parents gave it to someone when we left—like a rent-a-cat. Just as I was getting attached to the cat, it was gone with no explanation. The same thing happened when we vacationed on Great Neck, Long Island. There are pictures of me playing with chicks and kittens, but at the end of the summer, they were gone right before we were.

Tinker was put in the kitchen and not allowed in my room or the rest of the house until my father left for work. Jackson or one of the staff would take him out of the building for walks. On rare occasions, my mother and I might also take Tinker for a walk. I really don't remember him ever liking me; he essentially became my mother's dog. Tinker must have sensed that my father did not want him and gravitated toward my mother, who doted on him. Mom had the most contact with the dog, so years later when Tinker died in her arms, at a ripe old age, she was hysterical and grief-stricken.

Sammy Davis came over a lot and was not required to use the service entrance as my father made many other African-Americans do when visiting him at the house. I think this was because Sammy brought in so much money and was loved so much by all audiences. I'm not entirely sure if my father was prejudiced or if he was just a product of the times. I saw Sammy perform many times at the Copa; it was always thrilling. Sammy Davis Jr. was always very nice to me; he was a real sweetheart and so very talented.

The Will Mastin Trio and me: Will Mastin, Sammy Davis Jr., and Sammy Davis Sr. all signed this photo to me.

JULES PODELL presents

...vis, Jr.

JULES PODELL PRESENTS

JULES PODELL PRESENTS

BUDDY HACKETT
MARION MARLOWE
TEDDY RANDAZZO
COPACABANA
10 E. 60· PL 8-0900
DINNER $3.50

THE COPA presents

DEAN MARTIN & JERR... LE...
In The New Summ...
For DINNER
THEN AT 12
COPACA...
10 E. 60 · PL 8-09...
DINNER $2

...0 E. 60· ...BANA
...PL 8-090
DINNER $3.50

...DEWOOD
...NTALS

after-d...
mo...
show wor...
at only a...
Copa bonne...

CHAPTER 4

The Performers and the Stars

In terms of sheer star power, the Copacabana generated enough to illuminate the city brightly, year after year. The collective talent that graced its stage over the decades was a who's who of the world of burlesque, vaudeville, Broadway, radio, television, movies, and music. No other nightclub in New York had such an amazing roster of headline performers. Jules Podell's Copacabana could boast that it was "New York's heart-quarters for great stars, great stars on the stage and at the tables, for the Copa is the showcase of show business."

Me with The Four Lads during one of their engagements at the Copa. The group was from Canada and had a string of hits in the 1950s and 1960s including "Istanbul (Not Constantinople)" and "Moments To Remember."

Frank Sinatra, Dean Martin, Jerry Lewis, Peggy Lee, Nat King Cole, Danny Thomas, Perry Como, Jimmy Durante, Lena Horne, Joe E. Lewis, Tony Bennett, Ella Fitzgerald, Bobby Darin, Paul Anka, Billy Eckstine, Louis Prima, Keely Smith, Connie Francis, Frankie Laine, Sid Caesar, Buddy Hackett, Sammy Davis Jr., Desi Arnaz, Xavier Cugat, Eddie Fisher, Mel Torme, Phil Silvers, Vic Damone, Red Buttons, Carmen Miranda, Rosemary Clooney, Ted Lewis, Johnnie Ray, Tennessee Ernie Ford, Norm Crosby, Steve Lawrence and Eydie Gorme, Tony Martin, Jackie Wilson, the Nicholas Brothers, Martha Raye, Chubby Checker, Johnny Mathis, Mort Sahl, Sam Cooke, the Mills Brothers, Jimmy Roselli, Petula Clark, Joan Rivers, Pat Cooper, Tom Jones, Dionne Warwick, Jack Jones, the Temptations, Wayne Newton, Diana Ross and the Supremes, Don Rickles, Bobby Vinton, Jerry Vale, Gladys

Knight and the Pips, and Tony Orlando and Dawn all performed at the Copa.

It would be impossible to give proper credit to all of the great entertainers who appeared at the Copacabana in one book. With that in mind, we have decided to highlight a few performers who are forever associated with the famed nightclub.

Me and a friend pose with ventriloquist Jimm Nelson and his dummy Danny O Day. Nelson gain famed on televisi as a spokesperso for the Texaco Sta Theatre starring Milton Berle.

Ernie Kovacs poses with my father, me, and a member of the NYPD during a holiday toy drive at the club. Kovacs was a pioneer in the early days of television whose life was cut short when he was killed in an automobile accident in 1962.

1950s singing sensation, Johnnie Ray, sits second from the right with a group of friends enjoying an evening at the club.

My father with Nat King Cole. When Nat passed away from lung cancer in 1965 my father was devastated as they were good friends.

My father and Nat Cole with two friends in the kitchen during one of Nat's many appearances at the club.

Nat King Cole and me. Nat was a kind and caring man; my mother said he was one of the nicest gentlemen she had ever met.

To Malala
With all of my best Wishes
Nat King Cole

Copa advertisements in playbills.

My father looks on as Joe E. Lewis arrives on a horse to promote one of his openings at the Copacabana. Lewis was one of the most famous nightclub comics of all time.

Singer Vic Damone, my father, and comedian Joe E. Lewis sharing a drink and a laugh one evening. Frank Sinatra would portray Lewis in the hit film The Joker Is Wild.

Dad, Sophie Tucker, Joe E. Lewis, and Earl Wilson. Wilson was a popular newspaper entertainment gossip columnist at the time.

Sophie Tucker and Dad with an unidentified man. Sophie was one of the first successful woman comics of the nightclub era.

Tony Bennett

When he was a youngster growing up in Astoria, Queens, the glamour of the Copacabana must have seemed worlds away to Anthony Dominick Benedetto, even though Manhattan was only a short distance. So when Tony Bennett finally got the opportunity to play the famed nightclub, it was a dream come true. Bennett recently reminisced about his memories of the Copacabana and its owner Jules Podell.

The first time I ever went to the Copa I must have been about fourteen or fifteen years old. There was a little schoolgirl that had a crush on me and her father had a connection at the club. One day he took us there to see Jimmy Durante, who was headlining the Copa at

Me with a friend, Tony Bennett, and my cousin Natalie. Tony was also an audience favorite at the Copa. My father was a big fan of Tony's from the beginning of his career.

the time. The act was billed as Clayton, Jackson and Durante, but Jimmy Durante was the true star of the show. To this day, it is still one of the greatest performances I've ever seen in my life. We went backstage after the show was over and Durante was very nice to all of us. I was just a little boy in awe of how great the show had been and I remember thinking to myself I want to do what Jimmy Durante does—be an entertainer. That really got me motivated to start thinking about a career in show business.

The first time I played the Copa was in 1952; I was on the bill with the great Joe E. Lewis. He was a special man; he was so wonderful to me. I was just starting out and very naive at the time; Joe was already a superstar in the nightclub circuit. Joe would ask me how the audience was before he went on and I'd say they were a little

Me with Teddy Randazzo; I had a huge crush on him at the time. Teddy had some success as a singer but is mostly known today as being a very prolific songwriter.

Comedian Buddy Hackett dances with me as my mother looks on. This was during one of the many Sunday nights that my mother and I would go to the club for dinner and to see the show.

Buddy Hackett, my father, and Billy Martin with an
unidentified couple at the club.

noisy on that side or they were talking during the act and he'd say, "Don't worry, I'll take care of it." He also gave me some tips on how to handle the audience that I still use to this day. I mentioned to Joe that after the engagement I was going to work in Dallas

JULES PODELL PRESENTS

BUDDY HACKETT
MARION MARLOWE
TEDDY RANDAZZO
COPACABANA
10 E. 60 · PL 8-0900
DINNER $3.50

and Houston. He was such a gentleman that he wrote to the reviewers ahead of my visit and told them how much he enjoyed my singing. That was all it took; the reviewers were great to me because of Joe's letter. I'll never forget that he was such a wonderful man to me, especially when I was just getting started in show business.

Coming from Astoria, New York, and being a hometown boy, so to speak, I can't explain what a thrill it was to play the Copa; it was really big-time. Sinatra, Martin and Lewis, Peggy Lee, Nat King Cole—all the greats played there. The Copacabana and the Paramount Theatre were the two great venues to work in New York in the 1940s and 1950s. The Copa was unique because it catered to the money crowd, the gangsters, and the regular people . . . just like New York.

I remember plenty about Jules Podell. He was always a gentleman to me whenever I appeared at the club. I learned to talk with him before 3 P.M. if I had any questions because after that he'd start getting ready to open the club and began drinking and his mood might vary. He had a ring that he would tap on the table if he wanted to get the attention of his staff and everyone would jump when they heard that tap.

I first played the Copa after I had a few hit records and was first starting out in the business. I hadn't really learned how to perform yet; it takes about nine to ten years before you can become a consummate performer and learn how to adapt to the audience. That's what regretful about today's kids in the business, they don't have the time or places to hone their crafts like my generation had years ago.

For my annual engagements at the Copa I would have new orchestrations written by people like Neal Hefti, Don Costa, Marion Evans, and Torrie Zito. I tried to do the material I had just recorded or was about to record. I remember doing an engagement at the Copa in early 1958 that featured famous musicians Herbie Mann, Candido, and Sabu because we had just recorded the album *The Beat of My Heart* and I wanted to feature some of that material in the show. Once I established myself, I played the Copacabana regularly for almost twenty years. The Copa would book me a lot for prom season—that was one of the busiest times of the year for them. It was great because my shows all got wonderful reviews and whatever entertainers were in New York at the time would stop by to catch our show. I always made it a point to introduce the visiting celebrities to the audience sometime during the show.

The house band at the Copa was always good, but like other acts, I'd bring along key members of my group and usually had Ralph Sharon with me on the piano.

The shows at the Copa were actually like revues—the Copa Girls would open the show and a comedian and then a headliner usually followed them. It was wild because you'd have to do two or three shows per night. If you did three shows you wouldn't get out until four in the morning and you'd be numb.

Besides other fellow entertainers who would come by and see

Eydie Gorme's opening night at the Copa in September 1965. Tennessee governor and Mrs. Frank Clement along with Gorme's husband, Steve Lawrence, congratulate her after the show.

Steve Lawrence, unidentified man, Eydie Gorme, and my father toast another successful engagement at the club.

the show, the audience seemed to be made up of Jewish and Italian mobsters on the weekends.

Then the whole era of nightclubs began to die—there were so many places to play, but in the late 1960s things began to change. Many of the clubs couldn't compete with the salaries the casinos in Las Vegas were offering to entertainers. Times changed and people would be content to stay at home and be entertained by watching television. It was the end of an era. the Copa was glamorous.

The Copa was very intimate; it was basically a saloon. Frank Sinatra would say he and I were saloon singers. Clubs like the Copacabana were the greatest school for learning how to perform. It teaches you how to be very flexible since anything can happen. There can be all kinds of upsets: either someone is drunk and disrupts the whole audience, or a tray drops. All kinds of incongruous things can happen in a club because you are battling people who want to dance, who may have a business deal going . . . all kinds of interludes besides the actual performance going on. It takes about ten years to learn how to deal with these things because every night is different; you never know what's going to happen, so you have to quickly adjust to what the scene is that evening.

Joe Soldo, a musician who worked many of Bennett's Copa engagements, recalls, "One time, during closing night, Tony was so happy with the engagement and the band that he had the waiters serve champagne to the musicians. After Tony's last number, the waiters came up onstage and gave us all a glass of champagne; that was something special

because the musicians were usually treated like second-class citizens by the staff at the Copa, but Tony looked out for us . . . always."

Peggy Lee

"Her regal presence is pure elegance and charm"—so said Frank Sinatra of Peggy Lee. Lee was a staple at the Copa for many years, and her talent was a perfect fit for the club's patrons.

In her autobiography, *Miss Peggy Lee*, Peggy remembered her days at the Copa and Jules Podell with fondness.

> The Copacabana . . . I played it many, many times. It was a spectacular place and part of the reason for that was the way Jules Podell, the boss-man, ran his business. Jules used to say in his gruff voice, 'The mirrors are always clean at the Copa.' In fact, the whole club and the kitchen were always clean. I can't say that for the dressing room in the Hotel Fourteen next door, but the Copa itself was kept in top-drawer condition. All of the men, maître d's, captain and all, wore immaculate tuxedos and their shoes were shiny. The world-famous Copa Girls were known less for their dancing and more for their beauty. They would walk with their hands up and fingers extended as though they were drying fresh nail polish. Doug Coudy, the choreographer, used to teach them to walk in this manner. Three times an evening they dried their nail polish as they walked around the floorshow.

Phoebe Jacobs, a longtime friend of Peggy Lee, accompanied the singer to many of her Copa engagements. Jacobs recalled:

Miss Peggy Lee and me. Peggy was another one of my father's favorite performers—she always put on a great show.

I will say that Jules Podell treated Peggy beautifully when she appeared at the Copa. Peggy was on oxygen then and she used to get treatments, so she had to have the doctor come over from the hospital with the tank and all. It was a pain in the neck, but Jules went out of his way to see that things worked well and she was comfortable. Peggy did not like the fact that there were no dressing rooms on the premises of the Copa. The acts had to get dressed in rooms upstairs at the Hotel Fourteen, which was adjacent to the Copa. There was a service elevator that we used in the hotel and then a busboy would meet us and take us to an exclusive elevator that would take you down to the basement-kitchen area of the Copa.

So once you got out of the elevator you had to walk through the kitchen to get into the main room where they would announce you and then would go on the stage. Well, the problem was that Peggy used to have these voluminous gowns and they were frightfully expensive. In fact I remember one incident when Peggy was wearing a gown that I think Don Lopez made her and it cost maybe a thousand or fifteen hundred dollars. So when Peggy had to pass through the kitchen Jules Podell had all the busboys and all the service stopped and everything else for her to go through without ruining her gown. Jules would yell, "Here she comes, here she comes."

Peggy Lee continued: "Jules was relatively short and strongly built. His neck was short; in fact, he seemed almost all of one piece, one solid muscle. He drank a lot, but he always knew exactly what he was doing. If Jules wanted attention, he would knock his big ring on the table and everyone would come running. Tough? They don't come any tougher!"

Jazz pianist Mel Powell recounted the following story in Lee's autobiography:

Once when Peggy was playing the Copa, she was having a big birthday party after the show for Jules Podell. It was a pretty elite mob, including Tony Bennett and Sammy Davis. They were all at a long table with Peg and friend of mine, including Nick, the

Mary Ann Shedon, Peggy Lee, and me backstage at the club.

Africanologist, and his wife. It was the early morning hours and the joint was officially closed. We were having drinks, food, a lot of laughs and birthday greetings, and a band was playing off in an anteroom. Nick, the Africanologist, was absolutely bagged, and when he heard the band, he wanted to go into the anteroom. Nick, a big guy, knew his way around. Suddenly he was a little assertive, there was a commotion, and he came stomping back. Out of the woodwork stormed Jules's boys. This was a tough joint. It was like a George Raft movie, with all the boys in tuxedos. They encircled Nick. Nick was about to be undone when Peg spotted him. She got into that circle and identified him as a friend of hers, faster, more sober, and more serious than anyone had ever seen. Probably saved the guy from a bad beating. After all, they were protecting Peg, but she said to back off. For Nick, the protocol against letting yourself be shoved was tough to overcome. Peg had called Jules, and when he came into the center of the guys, she said, "The man doesn't know what he's doing, he's just drunk." Peg was the one. I didn't see anyone else pay much attention. When action needed to be taken, that dame is going to take it.

According to Peggy Lee:

Jules was very protective, if he liked you, and he also did good things in secret, which are not well known. One day he called me and asked, "Will you do me a favor, Peg?" "Of course, Julie, what is it?" "I want you to sing for some nuns." Here was a man who only took one day off a year, Yom Kippur, and he spent the entire day in a temple. Now he was asking me about some young novitiates in a convent! He said, "I know the young nuns would like to hear you sing. 'You'll Never Walk Alone' is one of my favorites." "All right, Jules, what time?" "I will send a car for you at six o'clock. Then I can bring you back in time for the show."

I was curious, to say the least. The limo arrived, I was taken to the convent, and the beautiful novitiates had nothing but good things to say about Jules Podell and how he supported the convent almost single-handedly. When I came back, he said in his gruff voice, "Anything you ever want me to do, Peg, anything, you just ask me." You can never tell about tough guys.

Here is a review of Peggy by Robert Salmaggi that appeared in the *World Journal Tribune* on October 30, 1966. The title of the piece was THIS GAL GOES BY THE BOOK:

We're gonna throw the book at Peggy Lee. When this gold-topped gal is being caressed with a baby-blue spot, and lofting the inimitable Lee sound, you find yourself admiring the letter perfect precision of her act. The lead-in cues, the accord between vocalist and band, the split-second timing of the soundman, and the click lighting liaison, are the constant envy of Peggy's songbird contemporaries. It's because Peggy goes strictly by the book. Literally. It's a large, black-leather-bound loose-leaf affair; jammed with neatly typed-and-mimeo'd notes and data, all lovingly compiled and looked after by Peggy's gal Friday, Phoebe Jacobs. If Peggy were to lose her "show-book" (and she did, for a few harrowing hours, just before a Copacabana stint last year), things wouldn't be half so sweet on stage. Peggy knows it: "That book is half of me—the better half." Even a cursory flip-through of the show-book bears Peggy out. Every show she's done for the past two decades, right down to each song she sang and what she wore, is carefully recorded so she can refer to the notes for a multitude of reasons ("Sometimes I want to revive a song or medley I did that went over with the crowd"). For any upcoming shows (her current engagement at the Copacabana, for instance) Peggy's book outlines, even to hand gestures, what is to happen on stage for

Me and Juliet Prowse. Prowse was a popular dancer who also starred in several movies including G.I. Blues with Elvis and Can-Can with Frank Sinatra.

An autographed photo to me from The McGuire Sisters. The trio became famous after they appeared on Arthur Godfrey's Talent Scouts and had several hit records, including Sincerely.

To
"Malda"
Sincerely
The McGuire Sisters
Chris, Phyllis, Dottie

her 90 minutes. She lists what sidemen she'll add to the house orchestra (half a dozen crack music makers always accompany her on tours), what numbers she'll do (with detailed side comments on treatment, etc.). There are specific instructions for lighting director Hugo Granata, the Copa producer Doug Coudy ("Diminish side lights at end of the song," etc.), conductor Lou Levy (" 'Pass Me By' gets a frisky beat," etc.). The entire contents of Peggy's 30-some-odd trunks are spelled out (Trunk Number One: Three pairs white kid gloves, etc.). There is no room for error, or miscalculation. Peggy goes about her profitable business with a shrewd, get-things-done-right attitude that has kept her sailing on the top of the vocal seas through thick and thin. One of the "thin" spots might have been the advent of the hard-driving rock and roll, à la Beatles, but not for Peggy ("I was worried—for about two weeks"). For her three weeks at the Copa, Peggy, ever the perfectionist, has "packed" Joe Mele's band with a rare bass flute ("The only item I carry personally"), a Hammond electronic organ ("For that wild, eerie sound"), four guitars, and a harmonica ("You can't beat the Beatles, you join 'em"). The band was put through seven full rehearsals before Peggy was satisfied, but not a bleat of protest was heard. Musicians dig playing for Peggy ("When she hits New York," said Phoebe, "all the great sidemen call her and want to sit in for her gig."). It is that way with anyone connected with the scene. When Peggy played the Basin St. East, the manager would close the place for five to seven days so Peggy could be free to change things around to her liking. She even got things she didn't ask for—two new wings on the stage, an enlarged, luxury dressing room, etc. "It's the same everywhere she goes," said Phoebe. "Like at the Copa now, where everybody from Jules Podell on down bends over backwards to please Peggy."

What's in store for Peggy Lee? "I want to write more"—she's

written over 500 pop songs, including "Mañana," "I Don't Know Enough About You," etc.—"and even more important step up my charity work."

Jimmy Durante

Although he is probably best known by today's generation as the storyteller in the animated holiday classic *Frosty the Snowman* (which is shown every year on television), Jimmy Durante was a top star in the nightclub circuit for decades. Because of his trademark nose, he was nicknamed the "Schnozz." During his career, Durante paired with

Bobby Rydell and my father. Rydell was a teen idol during the 1960s and continues to perform today.

several different partners to complement his act. But make no mistake about it, the "Great Durante" was always the star attraction. Singer-comedian Sonny King was Jimmy Durante's sidekick for over twenty-five years. Durante asked King to fill in for his partner, Eddie Jackson, in 1950. Sonny King had worked for Jules Podell at the Copacabana as a bouncer and eventually was promoted to bar manager. "I can't explain it. I don't know if it was spiritual, but we looked at each other and couldn't stop laughing," King said of his instant chemistry with Durante. "The audience caught on and they were laughing, too." A few years later, a top executive from the Sahara in Las Vegas saw King's act at the Copa and asked him to come and work at the hotel. King would move to Las Vegas and make it his home. Sonny King continued to work with Durante until 1980, when Durante passed away. Jimmy Durante was such an institution at the Copa that he recorded a live album at the club in the 1960s that is still available today on CD.

Paul Anka

Paul Anka was a rising teen star in the late 1950s, known for both his performing and songwriting abilities. In 1960, at age twenty, he had the distinction of being the youngest star to ever headline the Copacabana.

Anka's record company at the time, ABC-Paramount, decided to record a performance of his during his Copa run in July 1960. The intent was to introduce his talents to the parents of his current teenage fans. Recording engineer Phil Macy from Bell Sound Studios set up remote audio equipment in order to record Anka properly. According to the album notes, the performance from July 6, 1960, was edited and

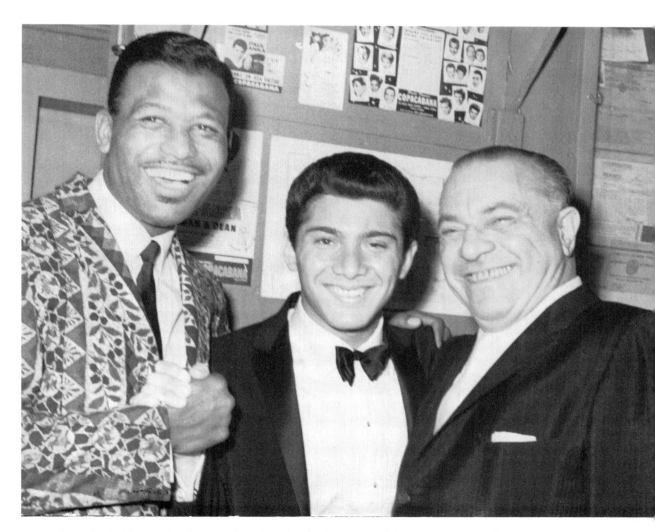

Sugar Ray Robinson, Paul Anka, and my dad. Besides being one of the greatest boxers of all time, Sugar Ray also developed a nightclub act and worked in television and the movies.

released as the album *Anka at the Copa*. The engagement was such a success that Jules Podell wrote Anka a letter that was printed on the back of the album.

On July 11, 1960, Podell wrote the following:

Dear Paul:

At the conclusion of your engagement here at the Copacabana, I wanted to let you know how we all feel about the two weeks you've spent with us as the youngest headliner in the history of the Copa.

We've had many stars with us over the years, Paul—some who were already well-established names, top-ranking artists who had become institutions in the business, others who were getting their first big break by an appearance at the Copacabana. I personally derived a great inner satisfaction in noting the rise of many a performer who was spurred on to stardom after an engagement here.

So you will understand my gratification now, when I tell that I feel that you are certainly on the threshold of greatness. During your engagement, I was amazed to see your terrific flair for showmanship, the natural gift for timing and delivery, and the sincere boyish charm which consistently characterized your performances.

You will be pleased to know that, for the first time in the history of the Copacabana, it became necessary to schedule three shows on the opening night of your engagement! The entire two weeks were most successful for us, and I think you continued to gather more fans and admirers among all elements and age groups as well as retaining the tremendous followers among the teenagers who filled the Copa so often during their "Prom Nights."

I was particularly happy to note that you recorded a series of your performances at the Copacabana during the two weeks, and that these will be released in album form for ABC-Paramount. I am

eagerly looking forward to hearing the album, which I will treasure
as a tangible memento of one of the outstanding engagements it has
been my pleasure to present.

Good luck to you always, Paul.

Sincerely,
Jules Podell

In 1962, The National Film Board of Canada produced a mini-documentary on Paul Anka titled "Lonely Boy." Jules Podell granted the filmmakers access the club in order to shoot Anka's performance and some backstage footage. The most fascinating aspect of this thirty-minute film is the interview with Jules Podell and the footage inside the Copacabana.

The first scene that involves the Copacabana is a shot of the outside awning, followed by a few seconds of the Copa Girls and the audience's reaction. The film then follows Paul Anka as he is getting dressed in a room at the Hotel Fourteen, exiting the elevator, passing through the kitchen, and greeting Podell. After kissing Jules on the cheek, Anka proceeds to light Podell's cigarette before heading onstage as he is being introduced by Doug Coudy to sing his opening song.

Wayne Newton

Another entertainer who owes a great deal to Jules Podell and the Copacabana is Wayne Newton. Television superstar Jackie Gleason was passing through Phoenix, Arizona, in the summer of 1962, on a train trip to promote his CBS network show. The owner of a local CBS affiliate television station was looking for an act to perform for Gleason

My father, Joe E. Lewis, Red Skelton, and a group of friends
enjoying an evening at the club.

while he was in the city for a luncheon. The owner remembered the Newton Brothers from an appearance they had made on his station and called Wayne to see if the brothers would be available. Wayne Newton and his brother jumped at the opportunity to perform in front of "The Great One." After the Newton Brothers had finished their act, Gleason was so impressed that he stood up and proclaimed, in front of the assembled luncheon audience, "You're on my first five shows."

On the September 29, 1962, the Newton Brothers made their debut on *The Jackie Gleason Show*. Wayne and his brother, Jerry, were planning to leave New York since they had no other work lined up after their appearances on the television show. When Gleason became aware of this, he vowed to rectify the situation for the brothers. Jackie called his old friend Jules Podell and asked him to book the Newton Brothers' act in the Copacabana lounge. Podell happily complied with his old friend Gleason's request and it turned out to be most beneficial to Wayne's career.

Wayne Newton always asked my father if he could ask me out and my father would say, "Yeah, go ahead." My father could have cared less about my thoughts. At that time, Wayne was fat, nerdy, and had a high-pitched voice, but finally I agreed to go out with him. One evening it was arranged that he would come to the house to pick me up. He arrived on time and spoke with my mother for a few minutes and then we went to dinner. The thing that turned me off about Wayne most was his ego; he was so into himself. The entire conversation centered on his career and what his future plans in show business were. He bored me to death telling me "I'm" going to be big someday and "I'm" going to do this and "I'm" going to do that . . . it was all me, me, me, me. After twenty minutes of this, I told him I was not feeling well and asked him

My father and actor Gabby Hayes. Gabby appeared in many Western movies as a sidekick, usually to Roy Rogers or Gene Autry.

Ad for D'Aldo Romano, a singer who never became a big star in America.

to take me home. Ever the gentleman, he took me home and offered to escort me upstairs to our apartment. I told him thanks but I would be fine. As soon as I walked in the door, I called another guy whom I really liked and told him I was now available that evening to go out.

While working in the lounge, Copa regular Bobby Darin caught the Newton Brothers' act one evening. At this stage in his career, Darin wanted to become a record producer and he thought that a song that had been written for him would be perfect for Wayne. The song was "Danke Schoen," and in the spring of 1963, Darin convinced Wayne to record it. The song and recording would change Wayne Newton's career and life forever.

Wayne wrote in his autobiography, *Once Before I Go*, that "Bobby was absolutely like the older brother I had always wanted." He also said of Bobby that he "represented to me the epitome of what I considered a

recording artist to be . . . he was the most consummate talent I had ever known."

Like many other entertainers, Wayne Newton would eventually travel to Las Vegas, where he became a top attraction, and still performs to this day. Newton has had one of the longest tenures as a headliner in the city, all thanks to a little help from Jackie Gleason and Jules Podell.

Bobby Darin

Although Bobby Darin, born Walden Robert Cassotto, died tragically at the age of thirty-seven in 1973 from a lifelong illness, his engagements at the Copacabana are legendary.

Darin first played the Copa in 1960 and at that point in his career he had a few hits on the charts, including "Splish Splash," and had played Las Vegas with comedian George Burns. Darin was enjoying success on the touring circuit, but he knew the Copacabana was the mecca of all nightclubs. Atco, the singer's recording company, had decided to record some shows during this engagement for future release. The resulting album, *Darin at the Copa*, continues to sell today, almost fifty years after it was recorded.

Bobby Rydell, my father, and agent Sam Branson in the Copa kitchen before Rydell's opening.

Darin's engagement at the Copa was a huge success; he broke all previous attendance records at the nightclub. The reviews were glowing and they catapulted Darin into superstardom as well as winning praise from the press and his fellow entertainers. Walter Winchell, a supporter of the young Darin, wrote in his *New York Mirror* column: "Bobby Darin's premiere at the Copa went down in the Copacabana history books as one of the Standouts." Martin Burden at the *New York Post* wrote: "Singer Bobby Darin is giving the Copa it biggest, boomingest business in years." And Gene Knight at the *New York Journal-American* summed it up best when he wrote: "All those raves you've been reading about Bobby Darin, the boy wonder of Hollywood and Las Vegas, are deserved. He is the greatest natural nightclub talent to come along since

Sammy Davis Jr. Which Bobby proved last evening when he opened a three-week engagement at Jules Podell's Copacabana. Within seconds after Mr. Darin, aged 22, came on, you knew he had it!"

Jules Podell took an immediate liking to the up-and-coming singer, and based on the tremendous amount of business the Copa had done, he invited Darin to return. Darin would work the Copacabana throughout the decade and enjoyed hanging out at the lounge even when he was not a scheduled performer. Darin and Podell would clash when Bobby decided to stray from the traditional pop standard songs that had made him a star and ditched his tuxedo for a more modern look—an all-denim outfit. One of the biggest confrontations between Darin and Podell occurred when Darin insisted that Nipsey Russell, a

Singer Tony Martin and my father. Martin was a popular singer who also starred in several films. He was married to Alice Faye and after they divorced he married dancer Cyd Charisse.

black comedian, be his opening act. At first, Podell resisted Darin's request, but finally acquiesced, realizing the business he would lose if Darin canceled the engagement.

Even though his career was short, Bobby Darin will always be associated as one of the greatest entertainers to grace the stage of the Copacabana.

My father and Jimmy Durante were great friends. Durante is wearing the Copa Bonnet, which was an honor bestowed on the most popular entertainers who appeared at the club by my father.

The Copa Bonnet

Jules Podell and Jack Entratter wanted to find a way to honor the top headliners who appeared at their nightclub, so they came up with the Copa Bonnet. "The Copa Bonnet was an award given to those stars who had scored memorable successes in Copa revenues. It has been called the Night Club Academy Award, the Oscar of after-dark entertainment. It was presented as one of the most coveted symbols of success in all of the show world, and little wonder, for just take a look at only a few greats who have won the Copa bonnet over the years" or so said the Copa's press material.

The winners would have their photos printed in the Copa menus and handbills with a Copa Bonnet superimposed on the top of their heads. The list of those entertainers who received the honor includes: Frank Sinatra, Joe E. Lewis, Nat King Cole, Danny Thomas, Lena Horne, Dean Martin, Tony Martin, Paul Anka, Steve Lawrence, Eydie Gorme, Louis Prima, Keely Smith, Bobby Darin, Jimmy Durante, Sammy Davis Jr., Jerry Lewis, Johnny Mathis, and Joey Bishop.

Many artists through the years would use the Copacabana as a venue to record their performances for album release. Bobby Darin, Paul Anka, Jackie Wilson, Jimmy Durante, Sam Cooke, Marvin Gaye, Diana Ross and the Supremes, and Connie Francis are just a few of those who have released recordings that were taped at the Copa.

Sound engineer and producer Hank Cattaneo recalls:

> My first encounter with the Copacabana was in the late 1960s. Dionne Warwick was doing a recording there for Burt Bacharach and I was asked to survey the Copa and determine where to gain

entrance, place equipment, and provide general technical support. Given the Copa's famed reputation, my expectations were high. However, I was to be disappointed with the reality. Instead of the grand showroom I had seen replicated on many a Hollywood set, what I encountered was a nightclub with a basement entrance located below an unattractive hotel. Though clean, it was small and dark, with odors of the prior evening's meals. It was painted entirely in black, with fabricated white palm trees—far less than what I had expected. The backstage entrance was through the hotel lobby, which had a balcony that overlooked the check-in area. It was said that here on this balcony young waifs offered their services to waiters and captains to gain free entrance when some of the legendary performers were appearing.

A small stage managed to satisfy some of the greatest performers. Their working space would continue to diminish as waiters would appear, adding more small tables to satisfy late-arriving luminaries who demanded front-row seating. A table that started out as front-row seating could become back-of-the-house as the night went on. Less-than-distinguished guests, or those who had failed to adequately satisfy a captain's out-raised hand, were escorted to the infamous "Burma Road" area of the club—an elevated balcony to the extreme left of the entrance where one's table offered less than a commanding view of the stage.

These details not withstanding, the Copa had a mystique all its own. Famous for its fine French and Chinese food, it was when the place was occupied with patrons that it became alive. The patrons and the performers made the Copa and the allure of its name become real. The hustle and bustle of guests, waiters, captains, and celebrities created an excitement that suddenly would transform it into the magnificent nightclub it was famous for [being].

The legendary Jules Podell, a large imposing man, was the owner—though it was often rumored [that] he represented individuals who chose to be anonymous. He sat at a small table not far from the entrance; it was [from] here, at that famous command center, [that] all matters pertaining to the management of the club were directed: cleanliness, quality and quantity of food, the pecking order of seating, selection of entertainers, their starting times, their departure from stage, etc. A simple rap upon the table from his famous, large ring would signal the nearest captain, and waiters would scurry simply to avoid what would be the rich voice of wrath that he was famous for. Acts would shudder with concern when that ring rapped more than once upon the table. [At] a level loud enough to be heard onstage, he would signal his annoyance at a bad joke. Lesser performers were known to panic. Were they on too long, had they performed poorly? He was a figure [who] was as legendary as his famous nightclub; Damon Runyon could not have created a better character.

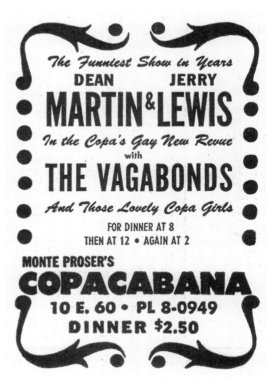

The famous Copa Girls, who often opened the evening's performances, were at times required to work in spaces not much larger than some tables. They were directed to the stage by a gentleman named Doug Coudy, who would often send them on their way with a loving tap on their behinds as they giggled out to the stage. Doug was the house production manager, electrician, and the soundman. He was, in fact, a "can do" kind of guy. The girls' entrance was at the foot of the steps, where all working personnel entered through the lobby of the upstairs hotel. Organized confusion often reigned in this area as waiters all

A night at the Copa.

served dinners from this location as well. Sound and lights were also controlled here. Doug, who had a slight but disarmingly attractive speech impediment, did his best to control the situation, but most often it was without success and at times could be quite funny.

One day I received a call from Paul Anka, whom I had worked with at A&R Recording Studios. He was performing at the Copa and asked if I could stop by to check out the sound. It seemed he was having some inconsistencies with the sound levels. The sound equipment, though dated, appeared to be working fine as I positioned myself in the show room during his performance. Still in view of the sound equipment, I saw a waiter with a tray of food pass by the equipment and, without missing a step, lowered Paul's volume control, only to see another waiter a moment later change it back again. Simple enough; I taped all the controls fixed to the correct level, and the rest of the show went flawlessly. Later, with Paul, I explained the reason for volume changes and what had been done to prevent it from occurring again. Though upset, Paul just shook his head in dismay. However, to prevent it from happening again, he requested I attend each evening's performance until his run was over. This eventually led to my touring with Paul Anka for many years.

Dad's famous ring; one tap would send shivers up the spine of the Copa staff.

My experience at the Copa, allowed me throughout the subsequent years to enjoy working with many wonderfully talented artists including Frank Sinatra. Those were the days.

Walter Winchell, the renowned gossip columnist, was a good friend of my parents. Winchell was also famous as the narrator on the popular television series *The Untouchables*. I remember him as an old man who smoked a cigar. Whenever he would come to our house he was always friendly to me. Winchell's wife liked the name Malda, God knows why, and they named their daughter Walda, after me. So her name was Walda Winchell. When I complained to my mother for naming me Malda she would say, "At least we didn't name you Walda!" After a while I said I was changing my name to Mickey, and I would tell people to address me as Mickey.

⌐The late comedian Joey Villa would recount this story about working the Copa:

> In 1962 I was booked at the Copacabana as the opening act for Nat King Cole. At that time, I was part of a comedy team called Forbes and Villa. When Nat Cole played the Copacabana for Jules Podell the place was packed . . . Cole was one of the club's highest-rated performers. One evening my partner, Don Forbes, and I were just getting ready to walk down the steps of the nightclub floor. Don was on the left and I was on the right side of the room when the announcer was introducing us to start the show. While he was on the side of the stage, Don started to flirt with one of the Copa Girls—which did not sit well with Jules Podell. All of a sudden, out of nowhere, Podell walk[ed] by and punched Don in the stomach; so hard that he was winded and couldn't even speak. By this time our names had been announced, so I was onstage for a few minutes alone before Don finally arrived huffing and puffing. Podell had rules in his club, and when you were at the Copa you better stick to them.⌐

Famous publicist Lee Solters, who has represented everyone from Barbra Streisand to Michael Jackson, remembers, "I had a client that was working the Copa, I can't even remember who it was now, but I went to the rehearsal. I didn't want to be noticed, so I found a seat by a table in the back of the room, figuring I wouldn't bother anyone in such a remote place. After five minutes or so, someone taps me on the shoulder . . . it was Podell. He says to me in a gruff voice 'Who are you and why are you sitting in my seat?' "

Rip Taylor remembers:

The first time I played the Copa was nerve-racking. I had finally graduated from doing my act in strip joints across America to legitimate clubs and then television. Someone saw me on *The Ed Sullivan Show* and that led to my being booked at the Copacabana. Meeting Jules Podell for the first time was very exciting. Before your first show, Podell would welcome and introduce you to the staff in the kitchen. I remember him saying, "Everybody, this is Rip Taylor, a brand-new funny guy . . . let's hear it for him," and the staff would all applaud. The acts always said hello to Podell before they went on because he would sit at a register in the kitchen and you had to pass him to get to the stage every show. I thanked him and was so happy my act was well received by the Copa audience. Although I had played the Latin Quarter and other top clubs, the Copa was special . . . it was the mecca of show business. I worked the Copa seven or eight times. Nat King Cole was, without question, one of the sweetest and kindest men I've ever met . . . he was just so wonderful. I can't tell you how it furthered my career, and others, once word spread that you had played the Copa.

Martha Raye would also visit us, and I would play with her daughter Melody. Raye was a popular radio, nightclub, and movie star whose nickname was "The Big Mouth"; later generations would come to know her from a series of popular commercials she made for Polident denture cleaner. Martha was fun to be around; she'd always sing and play the piano at our house. She could open her mouth so wide it looked

A billboard in Times Square announcing Sam Cooke's at the club. Cooke would record the live album *Sam Cooke at the Copa* during his 1964 engagement.

Me and two friends pose with Martha Raye. Besides being a very talented comedian, Martha was always very nice to me and loved being around children.

like the Grand Canyon. She was funny and a genuinely nice person. Martha liked being around children and always did something to keep us entertained. She didn't sit with the adults, she'd rather hang out with us. Sophie Tucker also came to the house a lot. I remember her being loud and fat, and my father loved her. Sophie would crack my father up; I never saw him laugh as much as he did around her.

Arranger and conductor Pete Moore recalled that during one of Tom Jones's successful engagements at the Copa, the singer had a request. After the first few days, Jones asked Podell if it would be possible to get some fresh lemons in between his shows. Jones told Podell that he liked to drink hot water with lemon to ease the strain on his throat. Podell said that he would be happy to have the lemons delivered each night to Jones's dressing room. Jones was grateful that Podell was happy to honor his request; however, he was taken aback when on his closing night, Podell had deducted the cost of the lemons from his performing fee.

Celebrity impressionist and comedian Rich Little played the Copa with acts such as Billy Daniels in the 1960s. During his debut appearance, Little's routine included a parody of the Sinatra (Frank and Nancy) hit song "Something Stupid." Little would sing the parody in the voice of President Lyndon Johnson, and one of the lines in the song mentioned Vietnam. One critic wrote a scathing review, saying how dare Little, a Canadian, mention the Vietnam conflict in his routine. This caused a firestorm of press and protests, which left Podell in quite a conundrum. On the one hand, the brouhaha over Little's routine was filling the club, as curious audiences wanted to hear the routine themselves. On the other, Podell did not like the negative press and protests in front of his club. Rich Little offered to quit but Podell told him that

OPENING THURSDAY MAY 1st

You've Got a Big Thrill

COMING ... ...

AS JULES PODELL & JACK ENTRATTER

Present

BILLY DANIELS

(BENNY PAYNE at the piano)

In The Copa's Sensational Summer Revue With

BOBBY SARGENT
HARBERS & DALE

PATSY & MICHAEL MADILL

PETER HANLEY · BETTY JOHNSON

And The Most Beautiful Girls In The World

MICHAEL DURSO AND THE COPACABANA ORCHESTRA

FOR 3 SHOWS NIGHTLY AT 8, 12 & 2

JULES PODELL	JACK ENTRATTER

COPACABANA

10 EAST 60TH ST · PLaza 8-0900

was not necessary. ♩In the end, after other critics came to see Little's controversial bit, the majority of them agreed that it was not offensive or disrespectful to the American people or the military. Rich Little would play the Copa several more times without causing any such controversy. ♩

As the decade of the 1950s was coming to a close, the Copa was still the "in" place to be seen. This *New York Sun* article, from 1959, on the nightclub scene in the city, praised the club as one of its best-run operations:

> The Copacabana, at 10 E. 60th St., is the only other major cabaret to give the LATIN QUARTER serious competition. It features a line of beautiful and stylish girls, picked less for their dancing talent than their ability to wear clothes, two dance bands—one for the Latin-America rhythms—singing and dancing soloists and one big-name star. Joe E. Lewis is a perennial favorite, and so is Jimmy Durante. Whenever they perform in New York, Nat King Cole and Sammy Davis Jr. pick the COPA for their appearances. Some of the beauties who graduated from the COPA chorus line are June Allyson, Joanne Dru, Janice Rule and Carroll Baker.
>
> ⌐The COPA is open seven nites a week the year around and is one nite club which puts an emphasis on good food. It has a special kitchen for Chinese dishes, which are popular with stay-up-lates.
>
> Like most every other nite spot in New York, the COPA has an interesting background. During Prohibition era it was known as the Villa Vallee, featuring (naturally) Rudy Vallee. Jules Podell, the owner, previously operated a Coney Island restaurant, a Fulton Street chop house, and the Kit Kat Club⌐ a

Ad for singer Billy Daniels. His most famous song was 'That Old Black Magic.' This was still during the time that Jack Entratter was working with my father at the club before moving to Las Vegas and becoming the entertainment director at the Sands.

late nite rendezvous where the BLUE ANGEL is now located. A friend who had returned from a visit to Rio suggested the name COPACABANA for Podell's new nite club when he took over in 1940. The first floor show was staged by Ramon, popular as part of the dance team of Ramon & Rosita when the Latin-American dances first came in. With his new partner, Renita, Ramon headed the show, but the vogue for their type of ballroom dancing had gone out and the early shows were flops.

Podell took on as press agent Mary Anita Loos, niece of Anita Loos, and now a well established writer herself. She proposed bringing in Don Loper, who danced with Maxine Barratt. Loper designed all of Maxine's clothes and she was the first member of a dance team to wear a hat and long gloves. Loper costumed the COPA girls in the same style, and that style has changed very little in the past 18 years.

Jules Podell usually puts in a full day at his club but seldom puts in a personal appearance in front. His club employs 275 people and his is one of the few restaurants where there is an employee pension plan for retirement.

The COPA is far more expensive than the LATIN QUARTER and its patrons are mostly big spenders from Miami Beach, Hollywood and New York. The name stars draw highly professional audiences.

Rip Taylor said, "Mr. Jules Podell made the Copacabana the premier nightclub of its time because of the acts he booked and the high quality of the staff and food at the club he demanded. He insisted that everything was perfect and it was."

Frank Military recalled, "Without a doubt, the Copa was the best nightclub in all of New York, or the East Coast for that matter, throughout the 1950s. All the top acts worked at the Copa. There were other clubs, such as the Latin Quarter and Bill Miller's Riviera, but the top spot was the Copacabana. The shows were productions, not just a singer or comedian onstage. The Copa Girls would come out and do a number or two and then the opening act and headline act would follow. There were usually two or three shows each night, depending who was headlining at the time. It was a great era that will never be replicated in terms of glamour, elegance, and entertainment."

A typical site in front of the Copacabana; a crowd lines up in order to gain entry and see the headline act. This night the Temptations were opening at the club.

CHAPTER 5

Bowlers, Brawlers, and Brooklyn Dodgers

The wonderful thing about going to spend an evening at the Copa was that besides the headliners who were performing onstage, the audience would almost always include celebrities, politicians, and sports figures who would sometimes be more famous than the star attraction. My father was always happy when someone from the world of sports stopped by the club.

Dad was a big baseball fan; I don't ever remember him being interested in other sports like basketball or football. I know at one point he played golf, but it was not very often to my recollection. His favorite team was the New York Yankees, and he would listen or watch the games

David Green delivers a cake to my father as he, my mother, and friends celebrate his 60th birthday.

Joe DiMaggio with my parents. Joe was a very shy man, however, he came to the Copa often as he enjoyed the entertainment and the way my father and the staff treated him.

Pee Wee, a Copa maitre d', Rafer Johnson, and my father in front of an ad for Tony Bennett's engagement at the club. Rafer Johnson won a gold medal in the 1960 Rome Olympics in the decathlon. He then went on to become a sportscaster.

Tonight, you'll hear TONY sing
"WHO CAN I TURN TO"
his latest smash hit
on Columbia Records

Dad with Clem Lebine. Clem was a pitcher for the Brooklyn and then Los Angeles Dodgers. Labine was instrumental in helping the Brooklyn Dodgers win their first ever World Series in 1955.

in his den before leaving for the club. T was a Brooklyn Dodgers fan, and I loved rooting against him. I have signed baseballs from the 1952 World Series, and he had a collection of autographs from the various players who came into the club. I wish I had them today, but my mother didn't realize their potential value and got rid of them when Jules passed away.

One happy childhood sports memory I have includes Sammy Davis Jr. Almost every year my father, mother, and I would go to the World Series games if a New York team happened to be involved. Jackson would drive us to the ballpark, where we would meet Sammy and his friends. Sammy's uncle and father, among others, almost always accompanied him as they were still all in the Will Mastin Trio before he went solo. I don't think Will was actually Sammy's uncle but they were very close, having been together since Sammy was a small child. We went many times, so I don't recall the exact dates we attended, but I do know the majority of the games were at Yankee Stadium. As you can imagine, with such a group, we were treated like royalty. Being a young girl, I really had no interest in the game, although Sammy would patiently explain to me what was happening on the field. The highlight for me was always the peanuts, popcorn, and hot dogs I was able to eat.

The baseball players and managers would sometimes come to visit our group and say hello before or after the game. I didn't know who the players were at that time, but I did get to meet many of the great Yankee players of the 1950s. Dad loved it when the Yankee players came to the Copa, and he would treat them as VIPs. I do remember meeting Mickey Mantle and Billy Martin and a few other sports figures at the club on occasion.

On the evening of May 16, 1957, a melee broke out at the Copacabana that would have a dramatic effect on the New York Yankees. That evening the nightclub and sports world would collide, and there would be no way to quash the story. Although the press was less invasive in the lives of celebrities and sports figures back then, this story was too hot to bury. While there has never been an accurate factual account that all agree upon and the participants' stories have varied, this seems to be what transpired that night at the Copa.

Several Yankee players who frequented the Copa regularly decided to meet at the nightclub in honor of Billy Martin's twenty-ninth birthday. Those attending the party included Yogi Berra, Hank Bauer, Whitey Ford, and Mickey Mantle, along with their wives. Sammy Davis Jr. happened to be the headliner that evening and a group of intoxicated bowling buddies began heckling him during the performance. According to those in the audience, the bowlers started shouting racial slurs at Davis. The Yankee players were livid and told the guys to sit down and shut up. After a few terse words were exchanged, the Copa staff appeared to have calmed everything down. While peace and quiet prevailed in the show room, it did not elsewhere in the club. One of the intoxicated hecklers would be found later, lying unconscious and with a broken nose, on the floor of the Copa men's room. Many believed the man had followed Hank Bauer into the bathroom, and Bauer took matters into his own hands. Bauer denied hitting the bowler, who later sued him for aggravated assault, but Bauer was found not guilty. The incident made headlines in the New York–area papers and around the country the next day. Several of the Yankees involved were fined $1,000 each by Yankee general manager George Weiss, while Billy

Jules enjoying the golf course.

Martin would eventually be traded to Kansas City. The Yankee front office blamed Martin for the trouble and believed him to be a bad influence on his teammates.

Mickey Mantle later recounted his version of what happened that night: "Two bowling teams came in to celebrate their victories. Sammy Davis Jr. was the entertainer. They kept calling him 'little black Sambo' and stuff like that. Billy and Hank kept telling them a couple of times to sit down. They kept standing up. The next thing I knew was that the cloakroom was filled with people swinging. I was so drunk I didn't know who threw the first punch. A body came flying out and landed at my feet. At first I thought it was Billy [Martin], so I picked him up. But when I saw it wasn't I dropped him back down. It looked like Roy Rogers rode through on Trigger, and Trigger kicked the guy in the face." Yogi Berra was quoted at the time as saying, "Nobody did nothin' to nobody!"

Billy Martin, Joe E. Lewis, Yogi Berra, Whitey Ford, my father, a friend, and
Don Larson. Dad was a huge Yankee fan and always happy when the players
came to the club.

CHAPTER 6

Jules's Legacy

Many people who encountered my father throughout the years saw only one side of his complex personality. Most of the stories repeated about him relate to his temper and tough-guy reputation. Despite this image, my father never laid a hand on me and hardly ever raised his voice at home. Don't get me wrong; his gruff exterior sometimes even frightened me. He was tough, strong, and could take care of himself in most situations. At the club he was a perfectionist and set high standards for the Copa; he was all business when it came to work and expected the same from his employees.

Handing out Christmas presents to needy children inside the Copa.

Musician arranger Pete Moore recalled a story involving Podell and a new employee at the club. One evening Jules spotted a busboy grabbing a half-eaten roll off a tray of food that had been returned to the kitchen. Podell approached the busboy and asked him if he was hungry; the busboy nodded yes. Podell had the busboy sit at the table in the kitchen area and had a waiter serve him a salad, steak dinner, and dessert. At the conclusion of the meal, Podell asked the busboy if he enjoyed the meal and the busboy said yes. Jules Podell replied, "Good, I'm glad you enjoyed it . . . you're fired!"

Danny Kessler, an executive with Columbia/Okeh records, discovered singer Johnnie Ray and signed him to a record contract. Kessler recalls Ray's first engagement at the Copacabana: "Johnnie was booked into the Copa for a limited run and he was a smash; business was booming . . . they had to turn people away. The Copa did not have an option on a future booking and Jules Podell wanted Johnny to return. Jules came over to my associate Bernie Lang and said since Johnnie was doing such fabulous business, there was a brand-new Cadillac outside for him and Johnnie would be playing the Copa again in two months. Bernie told Podell that wasn't possible since the Copa did not have an option and Johnnie was scheduled to travel to California to make a movie. Podell had his guys throw Bernie in the freezer at the club. Needless to say, Johnnie did return to play the Copa. Johnnie got along with everybody, including Jules Podell. What's interesting is that I went to Johnnie's rehearsal at the Copa and met a Copa Girl, Lynn Shannon, who would later become my wife."

Copa Girl Lynn Shannon Kessler remembers, "As a Copa Girl, we had to come down a few steps and walk through the kitchen to get to our dressing room and that was the only time I would see Mr. Podell.

Sometimes I'd wave and say hello to him, but I was scared to death of him for some reason. I was twenty years old and he had a demeanor about him that made me fearful of him; I'm sure it was a persona and he had another side to him, but I never saw it. I don't ever recall Jules Podell smiling; I didn't even know he had a family. Doug Coudy and Jack Entratter were the ones who looked after us Copa Girls; Jack was like a father figure to us. Jack took care of us and the other entertainers, he was a very nice and likable man. Jack was the buffer for Podell—it was like good cop, bad cop, and Jack was the good cop. Jules and Jack seemed to always get along, but we all thought Jules was the boss. I don't know why, but we all feared Mr. Podell.

In 1955 the building we were living in was going to be demolished, so we moved to the Hotel Carlyle, which I loved because I could order room service, for a few months. After leaving the hotel, we rented Frank Lloyd Wright's apartment and lived there for a few years.

As happens with most children, I rebelled when I hit my teens and didn't really care who my father was. However, there was one incident that scared the hell out of me. I was sixteen and had come home after a New Year's Eve party to change so I could go back out to another party. My date and I, along with another couple, left my family's apartment and went into the elevator. My mother was asleep and not aware that I was sneaking back out that night. When we reached the lobby the elevator door opened and there stood my father; I was terrified. It had to be four in the morning and my girlfriend said, "Oh my God!" I didn't know what to say except hello. He looked at me, said hello, and walked into the elevator after we walked out. As usual, nothing was said the next day about that late-night encounter.

In fact, my father never had to voice his disapproval, especially in the club. I remember once bringing an older date, whom my father didn't like, to the Copa. My parents joined us at our table, and after a few drinks, my date began to call my father "Dad," which was not a good way to start off the evening—trust me. Things got very tense at the table as my father just glared at him. I took the first opportunity I had to excuse myself to go to the ladies' room. When I came back to the table only a few minutes later, my date was gone. His place setting, drink, napkin, etc. . . . every trace of him had been removed. I never questioned it and my parents didn't say a word; we just continued without him. I never heard from the gentleman again. I'm sure he was quietly evicted from the premises—and all my father did was tap his ring.

Comedian Rip Taylor recalls, "One time, while I was working with Connie Francis, I rehearsed an eight bar impression of Roy Hamilton singing 'You'll Never Walk Alone.' Connie's father, who was also her manager, heard this and said, 'Rip, there is no singing on her stage.' I explained to him that it was only a routine, not a musical number, but he was adamant. I said, 'Okay, fine.' That night I went on and the audience reception went so well that they wanted more. So I say, 'Ladies and gentlemen, I don't have any more material, except one number I was asked not to do.' The audience starts yelling for me to do it; so I do the impression and sing 'You'll Never Walk Alone,' and as I walk off as the audience is screaming. Within seconds, Jules Podell walks into the dressing room and says to me, 'If you ever want to continue in this particular business you will listen when the owners tell you what to do and what not to do.' I apologized to Connie Francis, her father, and Mr. Podell; everything was fine for the rest of the engagement."

My father was very religious, but he attended temple only once a

My father hands out toys to orphans during the holiday season in front of the club.

My father hands out toys to orphans during the
holiday season in front of the club.

JULES'S LEGACY ✳ 171

year, on Yom Kippur. Mother and I would also accompany him. Since he was such a generous supporter of the temple, I doubt anyone ever questioned his sincerity or faith. The tradition was that you were supposed to walk to temple. We lived on Seventy-first Street and Fifth Avenue; the temple was on Eighty-sixth Street. The three of us would get in the car and have Jackson drive us to Eighty-fifth Street then drop us off to walk the rest of the way. It wasn't just us; we would see all the other good Jewish families doing the same thing. We'd arrive on time just like all the other families did. My father wore a yarmulke at temple, as all the other men did, and would worship downstairs. The women would go upstairs for the service.

The holidays were always eventful at our home, especially Christmas and Hanukkah. Even though my father was born an Orthodox Jew, we celebrated Christmas. Every year we had a menorah and a Christmas tree; my father would have the staff bring a seven-foot tree to the house. Like clockwork, Jackson would decorate it. I called it the "instant tree" because one day it wasn't there and the next day we had a beautifully trimmed tree with star on top in our living room. My mother loved having the house decorated, but my father put his foot down about having a holiday wreath outside the door; there was a mezuzah on the door. Although my mother converted to Judaism before I was born, she told me she even did the "mikvah" thing, she did not adhere to any of the strict Jewish traditions.

Mostly Jewish families lived in our building, but I think we were the only ones who celebrated Christmas. My parents did not associate with anyone in our building, and I never saw people in the elevator we used. There was another elevator on the other side of the building that I assume the other residents must have used. It was so private, we could have had animal sacrifices and no one would have ever known. I don't think Dad needed to worry about a tenant uprising because of a holiday wreath on our door!

On Christmas Eve there would always be a big party with a lot of adults. The air was permeated with the smell of perfume and cigarette smoke. In those days, everybody smoked either cigarettes or cigars. We had a piano in the living room and I remember people, especially Jimmy Durante, gathering around it to sing Christmas carols. Occasionally, other children besides my cousins, like Jackie Gleason's daughter and Jack Entratter's two daughters, would come over. I recall Dean Martin and Jerry Lewis at the house one Christmastime; Jerry would some-times play the piano and Dean would sing. The men always stayed by themselves in one room and, I assumed, discussed business. As the night wore on they would tell jokes, eat gefilte fish, and get drunk; they seemed to enjoy themselves. The women were always in another room gossiping, eating, and carrying on with one another.

Every Christmas afternoon the mother superior, Bernadette, of the Mt. Carmel Order, would come by the house with a group of or-phans. Year after year, my father would send Jackson to FAO Schwarz to buy bags of toys and have them wrapped specifically for the orphans. I'm not talking about small items, there would be bikes and huge stuffed animals wrapped for them, among other things. The children would be ushered in and after a few minutes begin to open their gifts. They looked like they were having more fun than I had had earlier. Mother Bernadette was always very friendly and would spend a few minutes talking with me

I was never exactly sure about my father's close connection with Mother Bernadette, but it may have had to do with a woman named

Yetta Burko. Yetta was employed as a telephone operator at the Copa. Yetta lived in Brooklyn and she suffered from cerebral palsy; Father supported her up to the day she died. Of course Yetta did not fit the typical Copa-employee mold, but my father liked her and hired her. Every year, we would get a Christmas card from Yetta Burko and I'd ask my mother a hundred times, "Who is Yetta?" Eventually I would meet her at the Copa, and she was a dear, sweet lady. It is because of her that I believe my father was very active in raising money for a cure for cerebral palsy. Throughout his lifetime, my father would receive numerous

My father presents a $5,000 check to Mother Bernadette and Sister Josita for Mt. Carmel's Home For the Aged. The money was raised in a raffle at the Copa.

plaques and awards for his work on behalf of the many charities he supported with his time and money.

At Thanksgiving time, my father would buy and give away hundreds of turkeys to underprivileged families so they could enjoy the holiday. He was involved with the Masons and also made sizable contributions to our temple every year. Phoebe Jacobs said, "A lot of people didn't realize that there was another side of Jules that he rarely showed to the public. He was very giving and helped many people privately; he also gave back to the community. During the day he very often would turn the club over to various charitable organizations and let them hold luncheons or fund-raisers there. I went to many of these types of events at the Copa and Jules would charge the organizations very little, if anything, to use the club. Inside the tough-guy persona was a man who cared for his friends and those in need. You might say, in reality, he was a soft touch with a hard exterior shell."

My father was very generous and dedicated to charities during his lifetime. While he and mother wanted to be looked upon as respectable in the community, I think there was a deeper reason for his philanthropy. He was very patriotic and proud to be an American. I think he felt he should contribute something in return for all the success he had obtained in this country.

My father was a very charitable man. Here he is with Mother Bernadette and Sister Daniel providing Thanksgiving turkeys for the Mary Walsh home in 1953.

My father receives a Grateful Tribute award from the United Jewish Appeal of Greater New York in 1949.

FEB - 1948

Dad hands Governor Thomas E. Dewey a check to benefit a New York City charitable organization. Dewey was the governor of New York from 1943–1958; he also was a candidate for the presidency in 1944 and 1948.

Sam Hausman presents my father with a Citation of Merit award on behalf of the United Cerebral Palsy Associations, Inc.

Danny Thomas, standing with my mother, was the guest of honor at a charity event held at our home at 910 Fifth Avenue.

Judge Gertrude Bacon and my mother, in the white hat, at a charity luncheon in April 1959.

My father and Jimmy Durante entertain children during a charity event at the club for muscular dystrophy.

CHAPTER 7

The Copa
Past and Present

The 1960s was a decade of turmoil, more radical than most. The winds of change had been blowing three years prior, in 1957, when the beloved Brooklyn Dodgers packed their bags and moved west. New York was no longer the center of the entertainment world, as many of the network television production companies and studios would follow the Dodgers' lead and relocate to Los Angeles. The landscape of performers and the music world shifted as rock-and-roll was beginning to dominate radio airplay and the music charts.

Jules, Frank Sinatra, and some lady friends.

My family was also experiencing change, having moved into a
new apartment located at 900 Fifth Avenue. My parents would have our
new home renovated to their specifications, which took over one year to
complete. This would be my father's final residence in Manhattan.

The new apartment was spacious and elegant. The building had a
doorman and tight security. My parents each had their own wing in the
house. This was by design, so that Dad could shut everything out that
might be going on in the house and conduct his business in private.

This newspaper item from December 1960 illustrates the change
in the attitude that the New York city police department and local politicians were taking with the nightclubs:

> Very few New Yorkers consider their nightclubs that important,
> but for a month now they have been hearing the din of a limited
> war over a twenty-year-old police ordinance that requires
> nightclub employees, from entertainers to hat-check girls, to
> carry police identity cards. A Citizens' Emergency Committee
> has filled the air with charges of abuses and shakedowns; the
> cops have retaliated by combing the cabarets for cardless
> offenders. This week Jules Podell's Copacabana loses its cabaret
> license for a knuckle-rapping four days, and Sherman Billingsley's
> Stork Club is fighting a similar suspension. To many New
> Yorkers, all this was only a reminder (or revelation) that their
> city is the most prodigious nightclub town on earth, with some
> 1,200 licensed cabarets.

Although rock acts were now more common on the Copa stage
than before, there was still a huge demand for the great song stylists
such as Rosemary Clooney. This review by Bob Thompson on April 11,
1962, appeared during Rosemary's debut engagement at the Copa:

*My parents at the bar in the lounge area of the Copacabana. My mother
would have dinner with my father every Sunday night at the club.*

Rosemary Clooney, a staple of the singing field, peculiarly enough until now has never played the Jules Podell flagship, long regarded as one of the important display dates for singers. She has made up for this, of course, by bookings at the Waldorf-Astoria, plus a string of disk hits some years ago, which established her reputation. Miss Clooney still excels in many fields of vocal endeavor. One of her major assets is her flawless diction. Every word she utters is understood, even onto the far reaches of the Burma Road sections of the room. Of course, the how-now-brown-cow attributes are projected by a clear set of pipes. Technically, she's well in command and easily infuses warmth and feeling to her efforts. Miss Clooney purveys a series of tunes that have seen service for many years including recounting of her days as a hit-disk singer. She makes it an enjoyable session. There are times when she tends to use the woman's prerogative and talk too much, far beyond what is necessary to rest her pipes. But overall, she makes an extremely likeable impression, and at her late evening premiere night got vocal acclaim after a 45-minute wing.

Years later, Clooney would fondly recall the evenings she spent at the Copa along with memories of seeing Frank Sinatra at the club. "If you were really lucky and Sinatra was in town, he would sometimes do a third show at the Copacabana, at maybe two o'clock in the morning, and just sing ballads."

Acts such as Frank Sinatra were no longer the mainstay in terms of headliners. Rock and Motown acts, now the rage on the music charts, were being booked into the club along with stand-up comedians. The Temptations were a frequent booking in the 1960s and the reviews were good. One reviewer wrote: "The Temptations, Gordy Records group, opened at the Copacabana with a fast-paced fun-filled 60-minute show. The five-member team has perfected the art of showman-ship . . . backed by its own group of musicians, artfully integrated with the Copa's house band; the group, with the relentless energy of a rail-road express, delivered a repertoire of songs that included many of the top hits from their two latest albums, *Psychedelic Shack* and *Puzzle People.*" Although business was good, it was disheartening to my father, who certainly did not have a copy of *Psychedelic Shack* in his personal record collection. The times were changing and Dad was forced to adapt so the Copa was relevant with the current generation.

Gladys Knight recalled an incident with my father over her group's name, "The Pips," when she played the Copa for the first time. "We gave ourselves that name, Pips, in honor of a cousin of ours. His nickname was Pip, and he just did everything for the group. As a matter of fact, when we finally got an opportunity to play the Copacabana, Jules Podell, who was a big man in the industry at that time, wanted us to change our name. He said, 'I don't see having "Pips" in the Copaca-bana!' And you know what? We refused to change our name! Berry Gordy talked to us about it, too. He said, 'You've gotta be out of your mind!' and we said, 'That's what we came up with, take it or leave it!' "

Della Resse was an audience favorite every time she appeared at the Copa. Phoebe Jacobs said, "The Copa was still swinging in the late 1960s. One night Ella Fitzgerald and I went to see Della Reese. . . . I had worked for Della, periodically, promoting her records, and Ella and she were good friends. Ella was working at my uncle's club and after her show decided to go to the Copa and catch Della's late show. Della knocked them dead—her show was dynamite. Those were great days; after Della's show we went up to Harlem to have breakfast together; I loved those two ladies. There was camaraderie between performers;

they'd support each other; it is not like that today. I can't tell you how many celebrities would be in the audience at the Copa catching other performer's shows; it was something."

Edwin Starr was a black soul singer who had a few hits in the late 1960s; one was the song "25 Miles." One night my mother and I were sitting in our booth, one that my father always kept reserved for us, watching Edwin perform. His act was loud and he asked everyone to clap, audience participation, during one of his numbers. Mother and I didn't clap. So Edwin pointed to us and said, "You two ladies over there, why aren't you clapping for me?" My mother was mortified; she just froze like a deer in headlights. Word got back to my father, who became livid at Starr for embarrassing us. Needless to say, Edwin Starr never played the Copa again after that.

Diana Ross and the Supremes played the Copa at the height of their popularity. I went to the show and met Miss Ross. By this time, my father was not as fond of the many new acts as he was with the stars from the past such as Joe E. Lewis, Jimmy Durante, and Nat Cole. But as long as the new acts brought in customers, he was happy.

As the 1960s were drawing to a close and the decade of the 1970s beginning, the future of the Copa was not looking bright. The one bright spot for me during this time was in 1967, when my daughter Jama was born. As happens to most people, my father's last years were a mixture of happiness and sadness, mostly the sadness that comes with reflecting on days gone by. The Copacabana was facing some tough times, and the decline was rapid. Discos would soon be the new hot spots, and the era of elegant nightclubs was fading fast.

In 1969, my father decided it was time to eliminate the world-famous Copa Girls. Various reasons were given for the change, but in

Our family, at my father's booth, on a typical Sunday evening at the club.

the end it was a strictly economic decision. This clearly was one of the final nails in the coffin for the club. Customers no longer needed the extra bonus of seeing beautiful woman dancing and singing onstage; they were content with strictly a headliner to entertain them. A new line of girls called "The Golddiggers" attempted to capture the magic and mystique of the Copa Girls, but it was not to be.

Club patrons no longer had the patience to sit through a vast production show. It was not just the nightclubs that were affected by the change; for the first time in many years, variety shows were losing popularity and ratings on network television. New York was no longer the entertainment mecca it had once been; Johnny Carson would move his *Tonight Show* to Burbank, California, in 1972.

Also around this time, my father decided to cut the size of the house band at the Copa in half. Besides the monetary savings, many acts no longer required the use of the band, as they traveled with their own musicians or self-contained groups. Also, stand-up comedians had become as popular as the music acts and they did not require the use of a large orchestra.

The Copacabana and my father, for all intents and purposes, were now viewed as relics. Both were shells of their former selves. Although he would put up a brave front to the press and those around him, he realized he could not turn back time and that his world had changed. Because he could not match the salaries that Las Vegas casinos were paying the top entertainers, the club suffered and this made him very depressed.

He longed for the days when the audience seemed to be of a higher class and people would dress for a night at the Copa. At one time, men were not allowed in without a suit and tie, while women wore fancy dresses and were adorned with jewelry; it was very posh. The club had a strict dress code for many years, but that had to eventually be rescinded. My father did not like change, but there was not much he could do about it and he felt powerless.

Frank Military observed: "Clubs like the Copacabana couldn't succeed, mainly because of television and the fact that there were no new stars coming up as in the previous decades that could draw that type of audience. The public could see performers on TV without getting dressed up and paying for an evening out on the town. In the old days, if you didn't have the proper attire when seeing a show at the Copa, Podell would have you thrown out."

Over the next few years the club's entertainment schedule alternated between headliners and comedians. Sammy Davis Jr., Don Rickles, Bobby Darin, Joan Rivers, Bobby Vinton, Gladys Knight and the Pips, and Tony Orlando and Dawn all played the Copa in its final years. Tom Jones, a singer from South Wales, Great Britain, would for a short time rekindle the spark at the Copa by drawing record crowds during his 1969 engagement. *Variety* reported, "Jones brought a different element of excitement. . . . Podell's customers are ready for extreme volume as well as hard and driving precepts as laid down by a new generation which offers musical violence and validity." My father preferred the music of Sinatra, Nat Cole, and Tony Bennett.

Jama recalls:

> I remember my grandparents were always very regal. My grandfather was always in a suit or dressed well; they would never sit around the house in casual clothes. Everything was perfect at my grandparents' apartment; at that time they were living at a building on 900 Fifth Avenue. They had buzzers on the walls and

My daughter, Jama, performing on stage at the Copa with a friend.

under the tables to summon the help when needed. I even had a buzzer in my bedroom if I needed anything. After we finished eating, my grandmother would buzz to have the plates cleared by the maids. I was an overweight child because of my parents' divorce, so my grandmother would march me into my grandfather's master bathroom every morning to be weighed on his scale. My grandmother was very much into appearance and how things looked to the outside world. They wanted things to be just perfect all the time.

I was never allowed in my grandfather's bedroom, which was a little further off the den; that was off-limits to me. If you went further down the hall there was another huge bedroom with a massive walk-in closet that I would sometimes hide in. I would play with my toys or watch television in my grandfather's den. Since he was hardly home during the hours I was up, I made his office my room. I liked to sit at his desk and draw pictures in my coloring book.

Anytime we would go to the Copa, we'd always enter through the kitchen, never through the front door. I would be dressed up to go to the club, usually wearing my long dress and white gloves. I always took a nap in the afternoon before going to the Copa because it was going to be a long night out for me. I actually sang at the Copa when I was four years old.

In 1972 Jules made another radical change; he decided to close the Copa for the first time in decades during the summer months. With many New Yorkers leaving the city for vacations at that time, it seemed like a wise decision economically. The Copacabana was not the only club suffering from a decline in business. In fact, many nightclubs had already closed their doors or would in the next few years. The new generation was content to go to a club and dance to a disc jockey spinning records as entertainment. The future was bleak and this distressed my father. The main source of happiness in his last years seemed to be derived from Jama, his first granddaughter.

Jama recalls:

I have amazing memories of my grandfather. While others may have feared him or thought of him as gruff and abrasive, he was a gentle giant to me. Everyone seemed to walk on eggshells around him, but I never felt scared of him. The only time he was a little too rough was when we would have our picture taken at the Copa and he would practically choke me as he was hugging me. I would play dominoes with him when he was home and he'd let me take his order on the Copa pads, the ones the waitresses would actually use at the club, for his lunch. When we moved to Lancaster [Pennsylvania] we got a cat; it was a white Persian cat named Hector. My grandfather was not much of a pet person, but

My father and a group of friends.

when we would visit him in New York we would bring the cat along. Needless to say, Hector was supposed to be kept away from my grandfather at all times. You can imagine the tension one day when we were all sitting in his office and the cat jumped up on his desk. Everyone in the room froze but me, waiting for my grandfather's reaction. I'll never forget the way Mother glared at me. Because it was my cat, my grandfather didn't say or do anything and the cat was quietly removed without a scene. When it came to his rules, I had special privileges.

My second child, another daughter, Danielle, was born in 1972. I was actively involved with my children and tried to be a hands-on mom to them. Of course my mother thought I was crazy and would say so. She was shocked that my children were going to public schools. "I am leaving you money, and I want you to get a governess for your children. You don't know how to be a parent." I replied, "And you did?" I told her she wasn't there for me emotionally and that nurses practically raised me. "I went to your school plays, didn't I?" was her retort. She was shallow in that regard; she really didn't know better. The fact that she was so wrapped up in being Mrs. Jules Podell left little time for her to devote to me. She loved the fame; she'd walk in a room and everyone would dote on her.

By 1973 rumors circulated that my father might close or sell the Copacabana. Longtime friend and syndicated columnist Earl Wilson asked him if the rumors were true. My father replied, "I haven't sold out, everything is the same as it was, and, as I told you, I'm going to open in the fall. I don't pay attention to rumors, and don't you."

The tough facade he had built and polished over the decades, which served his position, reputation, and status, would soon begin to disintegrate. In the past, that facade vanished only for a few hours at a time, when he would lavish gifts on the orphans during the holidays at home or the club. Now it was slipping away as those he knew and worked with over the years themselves were either dead or retired and the club was on its last legs. His partner for decades, Jack Entratter, would hang on at the Sands in Las Vegas until he passed away from a cerebral hemorrhage in 1971. Entratter's status and position at the hotel had also diminished after the powers that be sold the hotel to billionaire Howard Hughes in 1967.

Even though things were tough for the club, my father was constantly trying to think of ways to keep it open and successful. It was hard for him to come to the realization that he hadn't anticipated when it was time to get out of the business and retire. It probably would not have mattered if he had, for the Copa was his life. My father had no hobbies; he had nothing besides the Copa. Nothing. So as the Copacabana began its decline and started to die, so did he. On September 27, 1973, my father passed away. The heart and soul of the Copacabana also died that day.

The day my father died was Rosh Hashanah. In the past, he'd never gone to temple on this holiday; he went only on Yom Kippur. Well, this day, for some reason he decided to go. Apparently, my father woke up and told Jackson to get the car ready, as he wanted to go to temple. My mother called me and said, "I don't know what is going on, but your father wants to go to temple today." So he went, and then he came back and they were sitting in the den and he said, "Claudia, I love you," then suddenly suffered a fatal heart attack. This was my mother's version of what happened.

Whether she was accurate or not didn't matter; I was thankful that he passed away peacefully; it was quick and seemingly painless. It seems he knew his time was coming and went without a struggle; he simple lost his will to live. His decision to attend Rosh Hashanah services that afternoon makes me think he had some premonition of his end.

It was ironic that hardly any celebrities attended his funeral; some sent telegrams, but that was it. There were photographers outside the funeral home, but it was really sad and amazing that with all of the people he had given a break to and set up, none came to pay their respects.

My mother did not last long after my father's death. He was the focus of her life, and when she lost him a big part of her was gone. Their life was a very strange love story. They loved each other in their own way. She was gorgeous; it was like Beauty and the Beast. I guess they were meant to be with each other. I still remember how she would sit there at lunch and would make sure that his food was the way he liked it. She'd just sit with him while he ate and then off he would go to the club.

My mother eventually moved to the Breakers Hotel in Palm Beach, Florida, where she enjoyed being treated as a queen until her passing in 1976, shortly after my son, Benjamin, was born.

It wasn't until after my parents had passed that I decided to try to track down information on my birth parents. I'm not sure why I waited so long; maybe I thought it might hurt Jules and Claudia. I was also busy living my life and having children.

As I was going through some family belongings, I came across my birth certificate at the very bottom of a box of pictures. I'll never forget that day; I was in my garage and I saw this birth certificate for a baby girl born on February 11, 1945, at Sydenham Hospital, New York. My birth mother's name was Frances Goldberg and my birth name was

My father and me before giving me away at my wedding.

Linda Goldberg. The paper stated that Jules and Claudia Podell had adopted me.

By the time I came across this information, my birth mother was dead. I would later find out that I had three siblings, a half sister, and two half brothers. After making contact with them, they informed me that we had a surviving aunt living in the projects in Brooklyn. My half sister took me to see my mother's sister Martha. The entire experience was surreal. Here I was in Brooklyn, talking to this woman lying in a bed who told me she had been with my birth mother the night I was born. Prior to that, my mother had been put up in a hotel and was taken to the hospital once she went into labor. All Martha recalled was that once I was born, my mother signed adoption papers and I was taken away.

I was still curious about how Jules and Claudia had made a connection with my mother. From what Martha told me, it seems that her sister must have known someone who knew my father or was possibly associated with the club. That "missing link" put them together to set up the adoption transaction to occur. I say "transaction" because my father paid Frances Goldberg, in addition to taking care of her hotel and hospital expenses. Since everyone involved at the time of the adoption is dead except me, the specific facts will forever remain a mystery.

Needless to say, my siblings did not grow up in the luxurious surroundings that I was afforded as the adopted daughter of Jules and Claudia Podell.

Time marches on, and while I do miss my parents and the excitement of the Copacabana, I lead a very satisfying life. Today I'm married to a wonderful man, and I have three wonderful children and I am a proud grandmother.

After my father passed away, the Copa would remain shuttered for several years. Rumors would circulate and items would appear in the press about the future of the club every few months.

In a 1975 interview, Frank Sinatra summed up his feelings regarding the nightclub era. "I do know that when the Copacabana closed, it was the end of a great era, of the so-called cabaret era, where all the names in show business worked. Everybody worked there; it was a great age at the time. There are no rooms in New York like that now . . . and there's no reason why there isn't a club like that in New York City today because every performer who works in Las Vegas would like to work New York at least three times a year. So figure how many people there are who would work—it would be loaded all the time."

While Sinatra could have easily filled such a club three or more times a year, most acts were not popular enough to do so. Also, because of the gaming revenue generated in Las Vegas, the show rooms were able to pay the entertainers a large fee in order to draw gamblers to their hotel casinos. Such was not the case in New York and clubs were unable to compete with the salaries offered elsewhere.

It was not until 1976 that the Copacabana finally reopened; this time it would be operated as both a disco and cabaret. The New York press praised the new owners and their renovation of the club and predicted that the new venture would be a success.

After a few years, the new owners of the Copa moved the location to 617 West Fifty-seventh Street. The club now catered to a Latino market. The Copa would again move, this time to 560 West Thirty-fourth Street, which had a larger dance floor and a more modern sound system. The weekly entertainment schedule consists of Latin salsa-style music and dance. Some remnants of the old Copa, such as the palm trees and tropical theme, remain. The club also does a brisk business as a catering hall for wedding and banquets.

In 1978 Barry Manilow would turn the Copacabana into a household name again with his hit song of that name. For the past three generations, the strongest link to the Copacabana's glorious past is that song.

Manilow recalled:

I went to the Copa for my prom in the 1960s; I think I saw Bobby Darin. I remember lots of palm trees and the beautiful waitresses there. For a young man, the Copa was all very adult. I never met Jules Podell. The Copacabana symbolized glamour and danger to me. The song was born when Bruce Sussman and I were on vacation in Rio and we were staying at the Copacabana Hotel. There were towels with *Copacabana* sewn into them all over the place, matchbooks with *Copacabana* engraved on them, signs with *Copacabana* blazing on them, and we were getting sun on the Copacabana beach when Bruce sat up and said, "Barry, has there ever been a song called 'Copacabana'?" I said I didn't think so. When we got back to the states, Bruce called me from his place in New York to my place in Los Angeles and asked me about that idea for a song called "Copacabana." I told him that I thought that he and his collaborator, Jack Feldman, should write me a lyric that would be a story song à la Frankie and Johnny; a story about a love triangle with a death in it; something you would see on television at 2 A.M. They called me back in an hour and read me the brilliant lyric to "Copacabana." I set music to it within a half hour and the song "Copacabana" was born. An interesting story: years later, I was walking down Sixty-first Street and saw workmen tearing down the outside of a building. As I got closer, I realized that they were tearing down the old Copacabana nightclub. I went inside and stood in the middle of the dust and beams; it was indeed the Copa where I had spent my prom night. I spoke with some of the workmen who recognized me. They told me that they were moving the Copa to Fifty-seventh Street. New Yorkers and I are family, and before I left, one of them folded up the Copacabana awning and gave it to me. I was so moved. I still have it among my valuable collection of memorabilia.

This song was also the inspiration for a musical titled *Copacabana*. The story of Lola, Tony, and Rico was set amid the nightclub scene of the 1940s where "music and passion were always the fashion." The musical enjoyed a successful run.

The Copacabana was a product of the twentieth century and the people who lived during it. Take a look at photos of Times Square a few decades ago; it was not littered with corporate coffee shops, fast-food outlets, and owned mainly by the Walt Disney Corporation. New York has morphed into a different city and the change, good or bad, began almost thirty years ago.

In December 2006 it was announced that the Copacabana would once again change locations. The current building that houses the storied nightclub has been condemned to make way for an extension of the number 7 subway line that will stop at the Javits Center.

It's hard to explain to today's generation what the Copa represented in its heyday. The elegance, glamour, and excitement of a night at the Copacabana were something special. New York, and that world, was a different place back then and the Copa was of that era. I don't believe there can or will be anything like it ever again. There are no more stars like Sinatra, Nat King Cole, or Peggy Lee, who could mesmerize an audience with just their God-given talents. There's also no one like my dad; it was people like him who made the

Copa so special. All in all, it doesn't matter who ends up running the Copacabana and where it may be located; it can never be the same. Regardless of the changing times, the club has lost its heart and soul—Jules Podell.

Jules Podell.

Special Thanks and Acknowledgments

I want to thank my parents for adopting me and my children for urging me to write this book. I also want to thank all my friends past and present for telling me to write this book for so long; especially Gina Barata. I want to thank my husband, Al, for his patience during the writing of this book. I want to thank Charlie Pignone for being my friend. I want to thank my daughter Jama for putting it all together for me and keeping me going with car rides to the city. Without you, all my dreams would never have come true.

—Mickey Podell-Raber

For their time and invaluable recollections: Tony Bennett, Barry Manilow, Rip Taylor, Rich Little, Frank Military, Phoebe Jacobs, Pete Moore, Lee Solters, Joey Villa, Danny and Lynn Kessler, Joe Soldo, and Hank Cattaneo.

For their time, effort, and assistance: Jama Vitale, Danny Bennett, Tom Young, Vance Anderson, Nancy Sinatra, Arthur Marx, Robert Finkelstein, Herman Rush, Ken Barnes, Holly Foster Wells, Ken Goldman, March Hulett, Johnny Pizza, Terry Woodson, Jeff Abraham, Craig Zavetz (TipsOnTables.com), J. M. Kenny, Bill Zehme, and Laurie Pignone.

Mickey, thank you for trusting me to tell your story and collaborate on this project with you.

—Charles Pignone

Matthew Benjamin and the entire staff at HarperCollins.
Randi Murray, our agent, for her belief and support of this book.

—Mickey Podell-Raber, Charles Pignone

Index